GUIDED TOUR TO THE AFTERLIFE

The Remarkable First-Hand Account
of One Woman's Death
And Her Adventures in a New
Life After Death

by

Harriet H. Carter

as told by

the late

Susan E. Wells

Hillbrook

2000

First Edition published by

Hillbrook Publishing Company, Inc.

P.O. Box 3308

San Diego, CA 92150-3308

TEL 858-675-8111

FAX 858-675-8114

WEB http://www.HillbrookPublishing.com

Publisher's Cataloging-in-Publication Data

(Provided by Quality Books, Inc.)

Wells, Susan E. (Spirit)

     Guided tour to the afterlife : the remarkable first-hand account of one woman's death and her adventures in a new life after death / by Harriet H. Carter, as told by the late Susan E. Wells. –

     1st ed.

     p. cm.

     Includes index.

     LCCN: 00-101866

     ISBN: 0-9678939-3-3

     1. Wells, Susan E. (Spirit) 2. Future life. 3. Spirit writings. I. Carter, Harriet H. II. Title

BF1311.F8W45 2000   133.9'013

                                                      QB100-335

Published in the United States of America.

Printed by Thomson-Shore, Inc.

Cover design by Robbie Robbins, Idea + Design Works, based on the painting, "Vision of the Afterlife," by Harriet H. Carter.

10 9 8 7 6 5 4 3 2 1

About the Authors

Harriet H. Carter, M.B.A., J.D.

A San Diego attorney with a practice in taxation and business law, Ms. Carter has had prior careers in banking and corporate finance. She has long been an advocate of the holistic approach to the practice of law, and her open acknowledgment of individual spirituality as the core of legal and business transactions puts her on the cutting edge of her profession. A student of metaphysics and other esoterica, Ms. Carter has published numerous articles on a wide range of topics.

Susan E. Wells, M.B.A., J.D.

A San Diego attorney with a practice in family law before she died in 1994, Ms. Wells had lived in Africa for a time in her youth, loved bicycling and sailing, and had a heart of gold both for her clients and for her many friends. Nearly everyone who knew her characterized her as adventure-some.

CONTENTS

III
ADAPTING TO A NEW REALITY

IV
NEW PERSPECTIVES ON LIFE

Truth is within ourselves; it takes no rise
  From outward things, whate'er you may believe.
There is an inmost centre in us all,
Where truth abides in fulness; and around
Wall upon wall, the gross flesh hems it in,
This perfect, clear perception—which is truth.
A baffling and perverting carnal mesh
Binds it, and makes all error: and to know
Rather consists in opening out a way
Whence the imprisoned splendour may escape,
Than in effecting entry for a light
Supposed to be without. Watch narrowly
The demonstration of a truth, its birth,
And you trace back the effluence to its spring
And source within us;

❦ ❦ ❦

Hence, may not truth be lodged alike in all,
The lowest as the highest? Some slight film
The interposing bar which binds a soul
And makes the idiot, just as makes the sage
Some film removed, the happy outlet whence
Truth issues proudly? See this soul of ours!
How it strives weakly in the child, is loosed
In manhood, clogged by sickness, back compelled
By age and waste, set free at last by death.

Robert Browning
Paracelsus

Dedicated to
Lillian Walker

I love you, Mom. Thank you for caring for me in my last illness. You are an angel. I feel your love in every moment and I know you feel mine. When your time comes, I will be standing at the end of the tunnel waiting to welcome you home with hugs and kisses.

Susan

Acknowledgments

To all who helped me bring this book into the world and offered me advice, encouragement, support, and love along the way—you know who you are and you know what you did—I thank you from the bottom of my heart:

Ted Adams; Loretta Barrett; Jim Beal and Roberta Shoemaker-Beal; Mark Blumenthal; Art Campbell; Ce Ce Canton; Jenna Cassell; Virginia Colburn; Norma Dillingham; Donna Eyman; Bob and Susan Hoehnle; Clara Hoehnle; Richard and Susan Hoehnle; Denise Kelly-Becker; Sue Lutz; Robin Masiero; Margret McBride; Wendy McPetrie; Joel Metzger; Cyndi Mobley; Laurie Monroe; Glenn Moss; Nancy Nelson; Gary Piepenbrink; Dan Podgornik; Ricky and Dawn Ridgeway; Robbie Robbins; Margaret Russell; Sydney Salt; Doug Sawin; Llizane Schmidt; Eva Shaw; Katherine Torres; LaWanda Tucker; Diane Walker; and Lillian Walker.

Preface

On Saturday, April 2, 1994, Susan Wells finally let go of her bout with cancer and died. To hear her family and the hospice volunteer tell about it later, she went out kicking and screaming, wailing and moaning, crying until she could cry no more. Finally, with a smile on her face, she simply stopped struggling and died, giving new meaning to the old expression, "Rest in Peace."

A few minutes after she was gone her family went out into the back yard and realized for the first time all day the sun had come out and the birds were chirping away, celebrating who knows what, but celebrating nonetheless. In about fifteen minutes the clouds rolled back in and it looked dark and ominous, as it had all day before Susan's death.

I had first met Susan Wells about three years before her death when I joined a group of women attorneys who met monthly to network and to provide emotional support to each other. At one meeting I was particularly frustrated about a case I had been working on. Susan approached me after the meeting and offered to help me with my case. She handed me her business card and told me to call her the next day. True to her word, she promptly returned my call and walked me through the intricacies of my case. I was greatly touched by her generous spirit.

Then about nine months before she died Susan showed up at one of our meetings and announced she was dying of cancer. Although she was apprehensive about going into that great unknown territory called "death," she was also surprisingly serene about it. Instead of to go in terror, she was determined to die with dignity and elan. She vowed to learn everything she could about this new experience, and she offered to share her reaction and insight with anyone who cared to listen.

We all went away from that meeting feeling sorry for our friend who was about to lose her life. But even more so, we were inspired by her sagacity and her spunk. If anyone could turn death into an adventure, it would be Susan Wells.

It was interesting to watch the reaction of those around Susan when they learned of her impending demise. Some were frightened by her "predicament" and slowly backed away in order not to have to deal with their own feelings about death. Others gathered around her more closely, not only to offer compassion, but also to assuage their own curiosity about the dying process and to deal with their feelings surrounding their own mortality. I was one who was attracted instead of repelled by Susan's imminent death.

My first experience with death came when I was five years old. My maternal grandmother came to visit, but unlike previous visits I had remembered, she stayed in bed all the time because she was sick. One afternoon my mother dressed us up and took us to visit Grandma at my aunt's house. Stopping outside Grandma's bedroom door, my mother and my aunt instructed my two older brothers, my twin sister, and me to walk quietly into Grandma's bedroom, to give her a kiss and a hug, and then to walk quietly back out again. We did as we were told. Grandma seemed happy to see us. Little did we know we were coming to say our last goodbyes to our grandmother.

A week or two later we were sitting at the dining room table and my mother cried all the way through lunch. She had just returned from my aunt's house that morning and told us Grandma had "died"—whatever that meant. A few days later there was to be a "funeral"—whatever that was. But we were not allowed to go because we were too young. I never saw my grandmother again.

My next experience with death came two years later when I was in the second grade. One morning as we were getting ready to go to school, my mother announced that Sandy, one of my classmates, had died on her way home from school the day before. She had run out into the road in front of the school bus and was hit by a passing car. But then the fact of Sandy's death was quickly overwhelmed by my mother's fretful warning that we should never, never, *ever* run out in front of the school bus. It wasn't until later in the day at school, when I noticed Sandy's seat was empty, that I figured out death must mean someone disappears and you're never going to see them again, for that's exactly what had happened to my grandmother two years earlier.

A few days later there was another mysterious funeral I was not allowed to attend because I was still too young. Afterwards my mother described the funeral. Sandy was there. "She was just like a cute little doll," my mother said. "She was all dressed up in a new red dress and she had lovely blond curls all about her face." They displayed her in a "casket," which my mother said was like a fancy box. I envisioned blond curly-haired dolls elegantly dressed in red lined up in boxes at the toy store. "So that's what happens when you die," I thought. "You turn into a doll." I had always wondered where my dolls had come from, and now I knew.

The following Saturday morning I was lying on the floor in the dining room talking to my mother, who was working in the kitchen. I was still trying to sort out my feelings about what had happened to Sandy. I had felt rejected by her on the school playground because she had always wanted to play with my twin sister more than she had wanted to play with me. I was ruminating out loud, "Oh, well, I don't care if Sandy *did* die! I didn't like her anyway!" All of a sudden my mother burst into the dining room and, with alarm in her voice, shouted, "Don't ever say anything bad about the dead!" Immediately I could feel Sandy's presence, as though my very thoughts about her had called her forward. Her feelings were hurt over what I had just said.

Thus another important revelation had come to me about death: You may disappear when you die, but you're still conscious and can travel around invisibly, hearing everything everyone has to say about you. At school I began to feel Sandy's presence even though I couldn't see her anymore. But I had learned my lesson. I never said anything bad about her again.

As I grew older and approached adulthood, I was to lose another grandmother, an uncle, a cousin-once-removed, and assorted school classmates to death. On the other hand, I eventually became old enough to attend their funerals. I learned they didn't turn into dolls after all, but instead were dressed up, made up with cosmetics, laid out to look as if they were asleep in a fancy casket, and then buried in the ground. The first thing I noticed was that people whispered when they approached the casket and most of them, especially the women, cried throughout the funeral service.

It was the crying that confused me the most. I could sense the presence of the people who had just died—usually they hovered just below the ceiling above us—and they always felt more happy than sad. So why was everyone crying?

Seeing the lifeless body in the casket, my theories about death evolved once more: When you die, you separate from your body and you go on living without your body. You get to come back and visit your own funeral, fully aware of what everyone is thinking and, best of all, no one can see you. "What a wonderful adventure," I thought.

My senior year in high school was an election year, and I joined a committee which organized a mock presidential election at school. As we were counting the votes after the election, we entered into a discussion about death. With a frightened look on his face the civics teacher blurted out, "I don't want to die! I'm afraid to die!"

Afraid to die? I had never heard of such a thing. "Why on earth would you ever be afraid to die?" I asked, incredulous that someone older and supposedly wiser than I would have such an attitude. "Because!" he retorted, equally shocked that anyone would *not* be afraid. Nearly all the others in the room rallied to his point of view before the conversation quickly switched to another topic.

In college I was to find the same attitude among my fellow students, among the professors, among many of my friends and relatives, and certainly in the news media. Even though most people had been introduced as children to the doctrine of an afterlife, very few were sure about it as adults, and fewer still wanted to think about it, let alone talk about it. People often joked about coming back to haunt their loved ones, but anyone who actually admitted feeling the presence of the deceased was considered odd, or even sadly delusional. Death after life or life after death—which was it? And why was everybody afraid of it?

When I was twenty-two my Uncle Paul died. Several months later I was lying in my bed drifting off to sleep when I was suddenly jolted awake by someone standing at the foot of my bed. It was a man wearing a plaid flannel shirt. As I sat up in terror, he evaporated right before my eyes into the dark night. He had looked like Uncle Paul, but I had never seen Uncle Paul dressed in a plaid flannel shirt at any time during his life. It *was* Uncle Paul though. Who else would have that wavy red hair and that unique grin? He appeared vibrant and healthy. And he was to appear at the foot of my bed several more times, never saying anything, only smiling before he would disappear once again into the darkness. In time I learned to be less startled when he appeared. I would simply say, "Oh, hi, Uncle Paul! How are you?" and roll over and go back to sleep. Satisfied I had finally openly acknowledged his presence without fear, he vanished as mysteriously as he had appeared, never to be seen again.

My several encounters with Uncle Paul represented a new breakthrough in my psyche. Until then I had only felt the invisible presence of deceased loved ones but, starting with Uncle Paul, I could actually "see" them.

Still, I was reluctant to talk about what I had experienced for fear I would be told I was crazy. The mental institutions were full of people who heard voices and saw things others could not. Better not to say anything about what I was experiencing. Even so, after Uncle Paul died, I developed an interest in psychic phenomena—or paranormal experiences, as they were sometimes called. What I was experiencing certainly seemed "paranormal," but I was also relieved to find out my experiences had happened to others too. Maybe I wasn't crazy after all.

When I was thirty-one my mother-in-law died after a six-month bout with cancer that started in her ovaries and spread rapidly throughout her body. The entire hospital staff was in denial over her condition and refused to talk with her about her approaching death. When I confronted the nursing supervisor about their conspiracy of silence, she told me they didn't want to "upset" my mother-in-law. I was shocked at their attitude. Had death become such a frightening subject it could not even be discussed with the person who was staring directly into its face? I read *On Death and Dying*, by Elisabeth Kübler-Ross, and found such attitudes were pervasive in hospitals throughout the United States.

One day my mother-in-law and I found ourselves alone in her hospital room. She turned to me and queried, "I'm dying, aren't I?" I touched her hand, looked straight into her searching eyes, and replied, "Yes, you are." She sank back into the pillow with a sigh of relief. "I thought so," she whispered.

From that moment on she and I had a special bond, for she had at last found someone to talk to. Sitting there with her in the hospital, week after week, doing nothing but listening while she poured out her heart about her imminent death was one of the highlights of my life. It turned out she was not afraid to die—instead she looked forward to it so that she could join her beloved husband, who had died two years before. But she was angry with the doctors and nurses, even with her children and grandchildren, who didn't seem to have enough respect for her to acknowledge this most important event of her entire life, who all silently pretended she was not dying when she knew she was. She hated it when she would start to talk about her impending demise, only to be briskly interrupted by an embarrassed, "Oh, Mom, quit talking like that! You're not going to die. You're going to be just fine."

This conspiracy of silence about her approaching death was even more painful than her cancer, she said, and she told me over and over again how grateful she was to have a sympathetic listener. As for me, I was glad to listen, for I felt as though I were being let in on a precious secret that had been kept from me all my life. Here I was, absorbing knowledge as my mother-in-law sorted through her feelings, reviewed the meaning of her life, and conveyed her courage to face the unknown that loomed just ahead of her. I commiserated with her as her cancer painfully ate its way through her body, and I rejoiced with her as she caught glimpses of a breathtakingly beautiful world beyond the pain. The closer she came to her death, the less she talked about the pain and the more she talked about this magical kingdom that she was approaching.

A few days after her first great-grandchild was born, and after we had sneaked the newborn baby into her room against hospital rules, she finally let go of her suffering and went off with her deceased husband, who had been standing patiently at the foot of her bed for several days waiting to take her "home." At her funeral, while everyone was sitting around crying, I saw her floating about, smiling profusely, even giggling.

For years afterward she would come forward from her world beyond the grave any time I thought about her. Sometimes I would only feel her presence. Other times I could actually see her as a somewhat translucent apparition. At all times I could carry on a telepathic conversation with her, seeking advice when I needed it, sharing what was going on in my life, and, most of all, feeling her love and gratitude for my helping to escort her through death's door.

Through the years I continued to be fascinated with psychic phenomena as I searched for an explanation of my ability to see and to communicate with those who had passed on into the afterlife. Nobody else I knew could do this, so what was it about me that could? It was only in my reading about psychic phenomena that I found there were certain people, called mediums or channelers, who could communicate with the so-called spirit world. I read about the spiritualists' movement that took over Europe and the United States in the 19th century. Famous literary figures, like Robert and Elizabeth Barrett Browning, Alfred Tennyson, William Makepeace Thackeray, and others, attended seances to establish contact with their dearly departed loved ones.

In the 1960's and 1970's psychic phenomena and communication with the spirit world became fashionable again. Metaphysical bookstores started sprouting up like mushrooms across the land. I read books by Ruth Montgomery, a former White House correspondent, reporting the activities of Arthur Ford, a famous medium who communicated with a deceased friend, Fletcher. In other books Ruth Montgomery described her own experiments with "automatic writing," wherein she would sit down at her typewriter and receive information from her own teachers in the spirit world.

Then came Jane Roberts, a poet in upstate New York who, with her husband, Robert Butts, and a group of friends, was exploring ways to develop her extrasensory perception. One evening Jane spontaneously began to channel an entity named Seth, who had known Jane and Robert in previous lifetimes. They scheduled weekly sessions in which Jane would channel Seth and Robert would take down Seth's words in shorthand. Throughout the 1970's and 1980's the Seth materials were published in a series of books explaining human consciousness, dreams, and the workings of the nonphysical realms we call the "afterlife." I read them all avidly.

In the 1980's, as I was pursuing my career in the world of high finance and going to law school at night, I continued to explore the psychic and spiritual worlds in my spare time. The channeling phenomenon grew rapidly, gaining national attention as J.Z. Knight, Jach Pursell, and others held seminars to demonstrate the channeling process and published transcripts of their channeling sessions. Robert Monroe, a former radio/television executive, published a book describing his out-of-body experiences and then established a research institute in Virginia to study these phenomena further. Raymond Moody, Kenneth Ring, and other scientists published studies of people who had encountered near-death experiences. These people gave glimpses into the afterlife that were strikingly similar to those that had been reported by my mother-in-law shortly before she died.

In San Diego a group of us began to meet regularly with Katherine Torres, who channeled Malachi, a delightful being, who had spent his last lifetime on earth as an alchemist in six-teenth century England. Week after week Malachi would regale us with the mysteries of the universe and counsel each of us on the issues in our personal lives, stressing the importance of our spiritual nature in the overall scheme. As Katherine Torres worked on a Ph.D. in metaphysics, she began to offer seminars to the rest of us to explore psychic phenomena and to develop our own skills in channeling. One by one, as we opened ourselves up to our spiritual nature, Malachi introduced us to our own spirit teachers and Katherine Torres taught us the techniques of channeling. Soon I had my own teacher in the spirit world, Ardrith, a being who had lived as a Cardinal in fourteenth century Italy, when the Plague was running wildly through every village. My friends and I would gather at each other's homes to channel our spirit teachers for each other, obtaining advice about our daily lives and seeking information about the universe.

It was through Ardrith that I practiced automatic writing, like my predecessor, Ruth Montgomery, only I had graduated from a typewriter to a computer. Through the years I gathered volumes of fascinating information about spiritual matters, about life and death, even about the mundane events of my own life as I embarked on a new career as an attorney. Through it all I maintained my fascination with death and the afterlife. It was with this background that I eventually met Susan Wells and took an interest in her when she suddenly found herself staring death in the face.

Every Saturday morning for about four months before she died several other women and I gathered at the home of Susan's mother, who had taken Susan in to care for her when she could no longer care for herself. At these Saturday morning visits we came to offer Susan our love and support and to sit and listen to her as she shared with us her experiences with cancer and her feelings about her approaching death. Over the months these gatherings started in the living room, then moved to Susan's bedside, and finally stopped about two weeks before she died, when she was too weak to receive visitors any longer.

At one of these visits I told Susan about my ability to communicate with beings in the realms beyond death. I offered to introduce Susan to Ardrith, Malachi, and my other "friends in high places," who would help her to make a new home for herself in the afterlife. I then asked her if she would be interested in coming back to tell me all about her new adventures. If we could establish communications after her death, I promised Susan I would share her account with her friends and loved ones she was soon to be leaving behind. We were all anxious to know she would be well and happy in her new life. Even more so, we were all curious about what Susan would find when she crossed over the threshold we call "death." Susan lit up like a Christmas tree and thought it was a wonderful idea. By the time she died this spontaneous idea turned into a mutual commitment to collaborate on a book about the afterlife.

Around the end of January, or a little more than two months before she died, Susan first mentioned to me she felt as though she could see into the realms beyond death. I reassured her that her experience was "normal," and I encouraged her to explore some more and tell me what she was seeing. Greatly relieved to hear she wasn't going insane, she mentioned these experiences to me several more times in the following weeks.

In addition, she started appearing frequently in my dreams as the weeks went by. On the morning of February 16th, at around 5:30, I was lying half asleep in my bed when Susan came marching right into my bedroom along with a couple of big flashing circles of light. I thought she was coming to bid me goodbye. Had she died during the night? No, she could not have, for someone would have called me if she had. I rolled over and went back to sleep.

When I asked Malachi and Ardrith about it later, they explained that Susan was learning to expand her consciousness beyond the boundaries of her body in order to explore her multidimensional nature. They said such out-of-body excursions were common among human beings who were preparing to make the transition we call death.

Later that morning I went over to her house and found her still very much alive. Moreover, she felt extremely frustrated that she was still alive and was becoming such a burden to her family. She wished she could leave her sick body behind for good, but she just couldn't seem to figure out how to die. There were times when she felt disappointed and a failure for not handling her cancer better. But then she would turn around and honor herself, saying she was doing her very best, and that was good enough.

As the weeks went by Susan continued to tell me she felt as though she were in two places at once, as if she were dying of cancer in this realm and becoming a baby in another realm. She also noticed she was developing new skills, such as being able to read people's minds and seeing auras around people and objects in her immediate environment.

Our visit on March 26th was canceled because Susan was too weak and in too much pain to receive visitors. The next morning I was awakened by the telephone ringing. It was Susan's sister telling me Susan was begging to talk to me and wanting me to come over right away.

By the time I arrived, the hospice nurse was there and had just given her a shot of morphine. I sat down next to her bed and held her hand until she drifted into a peaceful slumber. At the same time I called on Ardrith to watch over her and to keep her company when I could not be with her. He reassured me he often came to invite her out to play in the nonphysical realms and would continue to do so.

That was the last time Susan and I were together in this physical plane, but it would not be the last time I would "see" her. Shortly after midnight the next night, just as I was falling asleep, I was suddenly awakened by a woman standing in the corner of my bedroom. She was smiling, and she stretched her hands out toward me. Then I felt a wave of joy and ecstasy pass over me as she soared away. I lay half awake all night expecting the telephone to ring with the news that Susan had just died.

But she was not to die until five days later. I was sitting in my office working when the call came in from the hospice social worker that Susan had died earlier in the afternoon.

That night Susan was in my dreams—not as much the physical Susan, but the nonphysical essence of Susan who could not be seen or heard, yet whose presence could be felt. Over the next several days I was to feel her reaching into my consciousness quite often to say hello. At times I felt as if I were being observed, and I would hear snatches of conversation in my head, "Oh, so *this* is where you work. Oh, so *this* is what you do. Oh, so *this* is how you live." Her energy felt peaceful and joyful. She was like a child again exploring a new adventure, per- haps feeling as though she were visiting Dis- neyland for the first time.

The following Saturday some of Susan's other friends came to my house, and we shared our experiences with our "Susan encounters."

I was fascinated to learn all the various ways she was making herself known to her friends from her new realms beyond death. To some she appeared visually as a translucent phantom. To others she came through as a voice inside their heads, giving information only she and they could have known. One woman reported she could not see or hear Susan, but she had smelled Susan's perfume in her car. Susan's presence was felt by many of her friends and loved ones all the way up to the day of her memorial service on April 11th.

On the day of her funeral Susan showed up just after the service started. I saw her apparition as she floated in the side door of the church. She took one look around and smiled when she saw how many people had come to pay their last respects to her. Throughout the service I could see her flitting around, sometimes stopping to touch people, other times just hanging suspended in midair watching the service. For a while she came over and sat next to me, and then I could feel a jolt of energy around my right ear and in my hair, as though she were stroking my head to let me know she was there beside me.

After her funeral Susan disappeared and I went back to my usual work routine. But a week later she showed up ready to start communicating in earnest about her new life in the afterlife. I sat down to my computer, pulled up a blank page in my word processing program, closed my eyes, took a few deep breaths, and started receiving "dictation" in my mind, which I then typed into the computer:

> **It is with great pleasure and joy that I come to you from my new home in the afterlife. I want to share with you the great beauty and joy I found when I left my tired, weary, and sick old body behind and came to this dwelling place where all is light and freedom and peace.**
>
> **In our first several sessions, we are going to practice walking together in this plane of existence, so that you may see for yourself what it is like here. The reason I say this is practice is that we need to teach you a new and different way of perceiving our reality as we know it here. You will then be given an opportunity to come back to your realm of consciousness and translate what you have experienced into words, ideas, and concepts that can be understood by your fellow human beings.**

She then went on to show me her new home, a cottage by the sea that, she told me, she had created shortly after her arrival. In our second session she showed me a formal garden in the center of which she had placed two white wrought iron chairs. We sat there in the lush floral display and chatted like old friends catching up on each other's lives. On another occasion we took a walk through a deciduous forest fully stocked with animals, birds, and insects. On still another occasion we found ourselves sitting under a lone tree in a high mountain meadow overlooking a verdant valley that stretched as far as the eye could see. At each session we would sit there for a moment to enjoy the peace and tranquility of our surroundings before she embarked on her dictation for the evening.

As soon as she started on another topic, whatever scene we were in would disappear and be replaced with a scene commensurate with her discussion. There were sessions in which we would visit a half dozen or more such scenes as she bounced around from topic to topic. All the while words would flow through my brain and through my fingers onto the keyboard, to be captured in my computer.

In one of our early sessions Susan explained to me the process by which I was receiving the information:

> **I am going to take you on a tour of consciousness as we go along. I am experimenting with some different**

modes of energy modulation to see
which frequency creates the clearest
pictures for you in your mind's eye. As
I explained to you before, I can communicate best if I give you a human
physical perception of what I am trying to communicate. Thus, I can flash
pictures and scenes for you to look at,
or I can produce sounds or just transmit energy into your brain that you
recognize as words and that you then
type into your computer as though you
were taking dictation.

Depending on the amount of worry and
stress going on in my own workaday world,
there would be times when I would sit down at
my computer in the evening and wait for what
seemed like forever before I could feel her
familiar personality come forward. At one such
session she explained the delay:

The delay in getting started on
the writing portion of our project this
evening has a very important purpose.
As you have already figured out for
yourself, when you sit down and close
your eyes to connect with my consciousness, you must first quiet down
the chatter that goes on in your very
active mind. Otherwise you will hear

only your own chatter and not the chatter I am transmitting to you.

Now I want you to know, while you are quieting yourself down and going deeper and deeper into your inner psyche, we are working at this end to open the channel that connects to your consciousness. From my perspective on this side I am doing something similar to what you are doing. That is, I am going into my inner spaces and quieting my own mental activity. I am then reaching inward to connect with your energy as you are reaching inward to connect with mine. The connection is automatic, for when you think of connecting with me and I do the same, we are actually focusing on the same vibratory frequency. The process aligns our consciousness and allows it to blend. In that way, we can "read" each other's minds, so to speak. Thus when I begin thinking about what I want to say to you, you pick up my thoughts in your own mind and process the information through your brain system. You are then transcribing what I have transmitted through your keyboard into your computer.

Her communications to me began to resemble letters; that is, they usually started out with a brief greeting and personal comments, then went on to a series of topics she had chosen to discuss, and finally ended with an affectionate salutation. If I had a particular question or wanted her to expand on anything she had previously discussed, I needed only to think about it as I was sitting down to my computer to begin a session. She would then respond to my thoughts during the course of the session.

Sometimes there were periods lasting many months when I was bogged down by the demands of my work and was unable to find the time to sit down to receive a letter from Susan. She patiently hovered in the background, and then she was ready to feed me more information whenever I came back to this project:

> **Well, greetings, my long lost friend! I know you think it has been a long, long time since we have sat down together. But I want to point out to you that the length of time is on your side of the perceptual fence instead of on mine. To me, it is as though we never left the project at all, but our getting together for this session is a continuation of the session before this one. In other words, I don't have a sense of time elapsed between one of our sessions and another.**

Over time Susan's consciousness seemed to change. She would remark she was evolving to new states of consciousness that were completely detached from the linear structure and organization we human beings find necessary to understand broad sweeping concepts. I began to feel as though I were being handed jigsaw puzzle pieces at each session, and it would be my job to put the puzzle together. Moreover, it seemed like a jigsaw puzzle without the picture on the outside of the box to indicate what the finished puzzle was supposed to look like. True to form, Susan read my mind one evening and made the following comment:

In some ways, this may feel scattered, disjointed and terribly unorganized to you. I want you to realize your organization and logical flow of ideas from one point to another are a part of your reality, not mine. I will do my best to help you sort it all out later on. For the time being it's all going to feel like a gigantic jigsaw puzzle to you. We are going to play with individual pieces, and you're going to wonder if you or anyone else can make any sense at all of what I am trying to say. But, eventually, the puzzle will come together, everything will come into focus, and you will get the big picture.

After I had what seemed like a "book full" of information, I then started to organize it into the parts and chapters you see here. In doing so, I discovered some missing pieces to the puzzle and Susan filled them in. For the most part, the words you will read are Susan's words exactly as she transmitted them to me. I merely compiled the pieces into an organized whole, using transitional devices and other editorial techniques to add to your reading pleasure.

I share Susan's story with you for two reasons: First, I was curious about what happens when we die and, even more so, after we die. If you are reading this book, then you must be curious too. Susan Wells presents one perspective on this age-old question in her special correspondence with me. I share with you what I have learned from my friend.

Second, Susan has asked me to share this information with you as well. As she was facing her own death, she was curious about what would happen to her. She read every book she could find on the subject, but she found to her dismay that the information was not readily available. During her life Susan was a highly educated woman. It was always her belief that knowledge brought self-empowerment. Similarly, as you will see when you read this book, ignorance can sometimes bring disastrous results. We are all going to follow in Susan's footsteps someday and die in one manner or another, just as she did. It is time we take away the mystery (and the consequent fear) about death and turn this once-in-a-lifetime event into the opportunity of a lifetime.

And now we come to the disclaimer, which all good lawyers love to spring upon the unsuspecting: Susan Wells's experience represents only one perspective on death and life after death. Depending on your beliefs, your experience may be different. Take what feels useful to you in your own journey and discard the rest. When you have completed your own journey, we hope you will come back and tell us what you have learned. In the meantime, and without further adieu, here is Susan's story.

Harriet H. Carter

San Diego, California

PART I

COMING TO TERMS
WITH DEATH

Chapter One

Letting Go of My Life

I don't know exactly when it was I realized I was going to die. But I know now the complete dying process took almost two years. The breast cancer I thought was in remission from my earlier bout five years before was reactivated and had progressed for almost a year before I began to feel its effects. There was also a window of time in which my unconscious self knew the cancer had sprouted back up again, but I did not—or would not—see it in my conscious mind.

One day I was busy working in my office when, all of a sudden, I started seeing flashing colored lights and felt a jolt of electricity race through my brain just before everything turned black and I passed out. After several more incidents like this, both in my office and in the courtroom, I woke up to the fact that the cancer had come marching back into my life and had taken up residence in my brain.

I didn't see it coming because I was distracted by emotional situations that were occurring in my life. But I know now my unconscious mind was well aware of this underlying physical invasion and could have chosen to stop it or let it continue to grow. Even as the cancer reached the surface of my awareness, I was still at choice either to fight it or to submit to it.

I did not see it at the time, but I now realize I chose to prolong that last illness to give myself an opportunity to become an expert in one more aspect of living. As with everything else in my life, I wanted to understand the dying process in minute detail in all its various stages from full health to a total breakdown of the physical body.

As I was going along in the early stages of the cancer, I realized that, on a conscious level, I jumped back and forth between wanting to live and wanting to die. I gave new meaning to the expression, "She didn't know whether she was coming or going." Admittedly, I created more hardship for myself and those closest to me because of my dillydallying around over the course of my last year. Just when I and every-one else were reconciled to the fact that I was dying, I would turn around and perk up again. Then when we all thought I was going to lick this cancer for good, I would have a setback that would send everyone into a panic anew. There would be times when I would have a glimmer of hope that perhaps the next course of treatment would knock out the cancer and bring it back into remission. Other times I felt, if only I would try harder, I could use my own will to send the cancer away. But the cancer just kept marching through my body. Though living seemed more familiar to me than dying and ought to have been my preference, in the end, I realized there was a greater part of my consciousness that wanted to let the cancer take its course and let me die.

I cannot say I had any fear of death itself, for I truly believed in the pit of my soul that it represented ultimately the freedom from my pain. By the time I felt this way, my cancer had spread to other parts of my body and was leaving me with episodes of severe pain. The various treatments the doctors were administering were making me feel even sicker. It's sad to say, but the truth is that modern medicine seems bent on curing cancer by administering treatments that make you feel worse than what ails you. There came a time when dying seemed more comfortable to me than living.

There was also a part of me that was feeling frustrated with my life as it had evolved to that point, and it seemed easier to let my life come to an end instead of to go on. In other words, it felt better to conclude my life at that point and let it be complete as it was. I felt I had reached a peak; my life had been rich and fulfilling up to then, but it could go downhill from there. So I chose to leave my life at that point instead of to take a chance of falling off the peak and coming to the end of my life later at a much lower level of consciousness.

I realize now we create not just one blueprint for our lives, but many. There are many forks in the road as we go along through life. We can choose to pull out at any of those points or go on for another leg of the journey. I reached a window of opportunity in my life where I chose to pull out instead of to go on. Of course, when it was made, this choice was still in my unconscious mind more than in my conscious mind.

Thus my cancer created the opportunity for my unconscious desire to be fulfilled. But because I was also unsure about whether I wanted to die this young—after all, I was only in my early forties—the cancer provided an opportunity for me to change my mind and get back on the path again several places along its route. This is often what happens when people are miraculously "cured," in spite of a prognosis from their physician that their disease is incurable.

This process of moving from the first stage of shock and disbelief after I was told of my prognosis to the point where I came to a final acceptance of my approaching death took about six months. By that time I had been through a series of treatments in which I lost my hair, I lost perhaps thirty or forty pounds, and I lost my skin coloring. When I looked at myself in the mirror, I could see I was beginning to look like "death warmed over."

The hardest part of the dying process for me was having to give up all the outer trappings of my identity while I was still living. When I started the process of dying, I was an up-and-coming attorney with a great career ahead of me. Seeing the inevitability of my death and knowing I would shortly be living on "borrowed time," I began to reassess my life and to reestablish my priorities for the time I had left.

The first thing I gave up—and not without some regret—was my career. There was also some relief in that I was finding it more and more difficult to think acutely and to solve problems, attributes which were imperative in the successful practice of law. I was finding it very difficult to just get my sick body through the day, let alone be brilliant, or even just competent, as an attorney. The idea of enduring the stress that is inherent in the constant deadlines and in having to engage in battle in the courtroom became too much for me to handle.

On the other hand, my whole identity and a substantial part of my self esteem were tied up with my occupation as a lawyer. We are known by what we do. How could I go from a brilliant lawyer to a dying person without some feeling I was losing myself in the process? After much grieving I was finally able to give up my identity with my career and to let it be okay that I was no longer "working." I did this by choosing a new career: dying. Thus for the next several months, dying was to become my sole occupation.

The next thing I had to give up was my marriage, for my husband could not carry on his own life and give me the increasing care that I needed as my bout with cancer became ever more challenging. Had I chosen to stay in the marriage, I was facing the prospect of being hospitalized to await my death. But in my mind hospitalization was no better than a prison sentence. I therefore decided to leave my husband and go to live with my mother, where I could receive around-the-clock care.

Hence the essence of dying for me was the stripping away of all my identity as a human being living in a particular culture in a particular time and space. By the time it was all over, not only did I have to give up my career and my marriage, but I also had to give up my home, my social life, my freedom to come and go as I pleased and my opportunity to create the daily adventures of my life. I had to surrender my privacy, my dignity, all the privileges and pleasures of adulthood—everything I had been and that identified me as a human being, including all my physical capabilities.

On the other hand, I had plenty of time to mourn and to grieve all those things I had given up and to let them all go, seeing in the end none of them really mattered much anyway. My career, my worldly possessions, and my whirlwind of activities were not my identity.

That was a very profound and important lesson for me to learn. Although I had given up all those things that, in the past, I had thought identified me and described who I was, in the end none of them did. In losing all those identities, I still had myself. I was reminded of the expression, "You can't take it with you." As I understand it now, that expression does not just refer to your money or your worldly goods. It relates to your entire life: all the events, all the relationships, everything about you except the core essence of your being.

At first I worried about how others would react to the news that I was dying. People in the United States have such a phobia about

death. I was afraid to tell others because I did
not know if I could handle their shock and
horror at my predicament. I was feeling alone
and needed very much to sort out my
feelings, to share those feelings with my
friends and loved ones, to talk, talk, talk,
talk, talk, so that I could release my own
shock and horror. Would I drive everyone
away, leaving myself to deal with it alone
anyway? Even after the initial shock waves
subsided, how much could I get away with in
continuing the discussion of my impending
demise? Was this the sort of conversation I
could politely engage in, or was it taboo
because it might make others feel
uncomfortable around me?

I soon found, however, these concerns were
largely of my own making. While many people
at first felt sorry for me, I came to feel they
were expressing compassion instead of pity. I
found, too, that if I stayed with my feelings
and told people how this experience with
cancer and dying was affecting me and what I
was learning from it, they listened with
interest. They were inspired by my hope
instead of frightened or saddened by my
despair. In time my imminent demise became
a part of me, and once I had honored it and
fully owned it, I could even laugh at it. It
became as easy to talk about it as about
anything else that was going on in my life.

I am truly grateful there was no denial of my impending death among my family and friends. When it was out in the open and could be honestly examined and talked about, it seemed far less foreboding, both for me and for them. I realized, too, I had a wonderful gift to offer to my loved ones. In opening up to share my experience of dying with them, I was leading them on their own paths of discovery, forcing them to look at their own mortality and to deal with their own fears about dying.

The most profound gift that came out of my bout with cancer was that it made me focus on what was truly important: the relationships in my life. I came to an understanding with my husband I do not think could have occurred without this "tragedy" to bring us together. I bonded with my family in a way I had never done while growing up. It was a source of great joy to me that I could witness my entire family coming more closely together and, over time, weaving together like a fine fabric that could not be torn asunder.

At times I felt like a burden to my loved ones. After all, I kept living and living and living, becoming the Energizer Bunny of survival. Members of my family who had come thousands of miles across the country to say their last goodbyes were forced to spend the next several months waiting for me to finally die as promised. The "two or three months" my doctor had estimated I would live when he told me my cancer was terminal turned into a whole year.

Most frustrating of all for me was the long wait. After I had given up my life and resigned myself to dying, I was forced to live on and on. I had nothing to do but to feel my physical body break down ever so slowly. There were times when, if I had been given a choice, I would have opted for some form of assisted death. Once I had become ready to die, my battle with the illness and the pain became unbearable. Time seemed to stand still. I begged anybody who would listen to please let me die. I was like a child waiting for Christmas, only Christmas was a long, long time away, and this child was being forced to wait in a torture chamber.

In the end, I finally learned to let go and to accept my situation for what it was, believing I could not control the timing of my death anyway. I learned to live one day at a time and to accept the pain with as much grace as I could muster. One thing is for certain: My exit from the earth was the experience of a lifetime, and it stands etched in my mind as one of the most important journeys of my soul through time and space.

Chapter Two

Getting Ready to Die

One of the most surprising things I learned about the dying process is that death is not a single event. It may seem that way from the perspective of human consciousness because we are trained to focus on the physical reality alone and to ignore the other realms that surround us and permeate our physical reality. Therefore we have the physical evidence to "prove" death is a single event. You're alive one minute, then you stop breathing, your heart stops, your brain waves stop, and—boom!—flat line. You're dead. (Everybody burst out crying, please.)

But that's not how it really happened for me. What I experienced was a gradual evolution from one state of being to another over a period of several months. At first I had my physical focus, and in that focus I saw myself getting sicker and sicker over time, until I could no longer keep my body functioning. I went from being a relatively healthy woman in her early forties to a wasted away, bedridden, suffering being that just could not take the pain any longer. Everyone observing my deathbed scene will tell you I struggled and struggled for hours on end. And then I just stopped breathing, put a smile on my face and—well, *died.* They then had their expression of grief—and, I imagine, quite a bit of relief that it was finally all over—and then someone called the mortuary to haul my body away. End of Susan Wells. End of story.

But that was only half of the story. From my perspective—which was from the inside looking out—I started realizing my physical life and my physical body were only part of me, and a very small part at that. I became aware I was not just my body. I was much more. For lack of a better term, I began to call that other part of me my "consciousness." As my body went through its process of breaking down, my consciousness began a process of waking up. I realized there was a whole universe beyond the physical realm just waiting to be explored. From my perspective, here was my body that felt like a shell all around the real "me" that was inside. Over time that inside "me" started growing larger. I was beginning to be aware that my consciousness was sometimes leaving my body behind and was drifting off to other realms.

It was not apparent to those in my outer world that I was doing this. From the perspective of those around me, I was sleeping a lot, or else I was under the influence of morphine. Hence they thought I was unconscious more and more as time went on. The truth was I was becoming "super" conscious, not unconscious. As I faded out from the physical world and into the inner world, my consciousness began to wake up and I began to feel super awake and super aware.

At first I had a floating sensation similar to that which we all experience when we're drifting off to sleep. Then the images of this other realm would start to take over. For example, I would be lying there in my bed waiting for the darkness of sleep or unconsciousness to take over, and suddenly I would find myself floating in a brilliant light.

I realized I was experiencing a different sensation of light than I would experience just lying in my bed during the daytime. Under normal circumstances, there would be areas in my bedroom brighter than other areas, for example, where light was coming in the window versus light in the corner where my bed cast a shadow. In this instance, however, the light would be coming from no particular place but would be everywhere at once. It was a bright light, but not a blinding light. It had a feeling of warmth to it, but not the sensation of physical heat.

After a while I would drift back away from the light and travel back through the darkness until I found myself in my bed once more. When I would come back to my physical awareness in my bed, I would feel shrunken and less alive. The worst part of coming back to my body, however, was that I would forget completely the experiences I had just been having in this light.

I cannot pinpoint a time when I started being aware of this nonphysical dimension. Perhaps I started getting glimpses of it in my dreams. Perhaps the morphine played a part, for as the dosage of morphine kept being increased, I found myself having more visions I could not fathom. At first I thought the morphine was causing me to hallucinate, for when I mentioned one of these experiences to the hospice nurse, she said it was common for people to have weird dreams and hallucin-ations with morphine. But as time went on these visions kept becoming more and more clear, and they stayed in my focus for longer periods before I would swing back to my awareness as Susan Wells. And then I would receive another dose of morphine and off I would go again, waking up in a new world, feeling more alive than ever. Were these hallucinations produced by the chemical interaction of the morphine in my brain? At first I would have thought so. But then I began to think otherwise.

As my physical health was breaking down, I found myself less able to live in my body with all its pain. I therefore took the morphine as often as I was allowed to in order to escape the pain into sleep. But I was not truly "sleeping." I was instead "waking up" and taking my consciousness to these new realms I had discovered.

Over time I found myself leaving my body farther and farther behind while I roamed around in what I now realize was a layer of consciousness between the earth realm and the nonphysical realms of the afterlife where I presently reside.

At first these nonphysical realms seemed strange. They almost appeared surreal, especially when compared to our physical world. Sometimes I would feel as if I were falling down a long tunnel. Flashing faces would catch my attention as I drifted around in seemingly empty space. Other times I would feel as though I were in some kind of hospital or convalescent facility, and there would be these kind and loving beings who would be standing all around my bed humming the most beautiful chants. I would get hazy glimpses of other scenes as well, but I could not always comprehend what I was seeing. All were beautiful, however. I don't remember ever seeing anything frightening when I was on these excursions through the other realms. At all times I felt safe and secure.

But the colors! You should have seen the colors! Incredibly beautiful, the colors were unlike any I had ever seen before on earth and were simply breathtaking. They seemed so bright, almost fluorescent. The sensation was, "Wow!" They would fill me with such a joy and ecstasy, I could hardly contain the feeling. Floating through the colors was not only a visual experience but encompassed all imaginable sensations. It was as though the colors would sing out in the most beautiful melodies. They would touch me gently and softly, like the finest satin. There was this underlying feeling of warmth and comfort—a feeling of complete contentment—that provided a steady, supportive foundation. The colors would reach out and exude a love and acceptance that would fill me to overflowing. There was this sensation of being supported from all sides, as though the very colors themselves were alive and were concerned about me. Still other times I would be surrounded by clouds of color, and these colors would actually feel as if they were releasing my pain and healing my cancer. It felt as though the colors were caring for me and were nursing me back to health and to wholeness once more.

Strangely, I would come back to check on my body from time to time, and then I would feel myself shrinking back down into the physical world again. I would open my eyes and find myself back in my bed, and instantly I would think I had just awakened from a dream or even just plain sleep. When I was in my body, the other awareness would shut down entirely and I would forget all about it.

My excursion back into the physical world would last only until I received another dose of morphine or went back to "sleep" again. I would then pop back up into the "real" world, the world of my consciousness where my true self was, feeling super aware and super alive once more. From my perspective in the other realms, the physical world and my life as Susan Wells felt like sleeping or dreaming.

I did this dance back and forth between the realms for several months, and each excursion brought more and more expansion of my consciousness. What I found in the other realms was great comfort and nurturing, which provided a balance in my psyche with the pain and frustration I found in my bout with cancer. It was as though I were on a teeter-totter. As each day with the cancer brought me more despair, each day in the other realms brought me more ecstasy and joy, all of which served to keep me in balance.

But all too soon I would drift back away from these other realms and travel back through the darkness again, finding myself back in my bed, waking up and feeling trapped in the pain and the heaviness of my body. When I would come back to my physical awareness in my bed, I would feel shrunken and less alive once more. I would feel despair at the prospect I was losing my strength and the ability to control my body. Life seemed to drag me down, and I would feel positively oppressed by the burden of my pain-racked body.

As I was traveling back and forth into these other realms, it was difficult to describe my experiences to my family or friends. For one thing, I was afraid they would think I was just imagining things. For another, there was the implication it was the drugs in my system that were causing these sensations, that what I was experiencing was not "real." Yet I was having just the opposite experience myself. As time went on I was beginning to question whether my experience as a human being was real. Can you imagine that? Here I was, floating around in these clouds of brilliant colors, feeling quite content and peaceful, questioning whether I was hallucinating my reality as Susan Wells, lying in a bed in San Diego, California, having a monstrous bout with cancer slowly eating its way through my body. What a nightmare! I wanted to pinch myself so that I could stop this nightmare and wake up into my true reality, drifting around in the clouds as nothing but a wisp of consciousness. Now *that* was what seemed real, and the cancer scenario seemed like fiction. In time it began to feel as though this physical realm were the sleep state and that other realm with the loving, singing, healing clouds of color were the waking state.

There were a few people with whom I could discuss my experiences, for they seemed, first of all, to *believe* me and to take me seriously. Otherwise I would have thought I had lost touch with my sanity, that the cancer had not only spread to my brain, but also to my mind. But these people said, "Yes, I believe you. I understand you. What you are experiencing there *is* real. Go and explore some more and tell me all about it when you come back." Those words of support were the very words I needed and gave me the courage to go forward and explore the other realms further.

In time, as I began to feel more comfortable in the other realms, I stopped drifting around in the clouds and started discovering details I had not noticed before. I suppose my experience could have been similar to that which a newborn baby experiences. At first everything for the baby is just a plethora of sensations, and blurry sensations at that. But over time the baby learns to focus its eyes and to give meaning to what it is seeing. It learns to distinguish one sound from another and to find meaning in those sounds. It learns to distinguish one physical sensation from another and to react to those various sensations. But at first it is just drifting along, not quite understanding what is going on. That is what I was feeling. I was just drifting along trying to figure out what I was experiencing. Then I started to become aware of patterns. I learned to distinguish one sensation from another. I started to see that I could manipulate some of those sensations, to make them happen or to make them stop happening.

So you might say, while I was lying there dying of cancer in one realm, I was a baby in another realm. I was drifting back and forth between the physical and the nonphysical realms for a long, long time before I "died." Flicker off as Susan Wells, flicker on as this new being—a being that did not even have a name, but a being nonetheless, and a being becoming aware of itself, discovering who it was and what it was and where it was.

What finally convinced me this other reality was not just a series of hallucinations was that I started becoming aware of other beings around me. At first I seemed to be just floating around in the light, interacting with the colors, feeling comfort from the love. But then I began to notice hazy shapes moving around. Sometimes there would be a pinpoint of bright light or perhaps a black dot in the distance that would disappear again leaving me to wonder if I had seen anything at all. Other times I would get the sensation of voices calling to me. Just as my first experiences in the light seemed to flicker in and out of my awareness, these other beings at first were flickering in and out. Was I really seeing them, or were they just phantoms and figments of my imagination? Was it just wishful thinking that there would be others there with me?

In time (and I use that term quite loosely, for I was not truly aware of the passage of time in these experiences) my consciousness evolved further. I had at first questioned these sparks of light and these wispy phantoms. But then they began to come into focus until I could say to myself, "Yes, these *are* real. There really *is* somebody here. I'm not alone."

When I began to believe these beings were real, they came into focus even more, and they seemed pleased I had recognized their presence. It was as though they would not intrude on my solitude but would stand by patiently waiting for me to invite them into my presence. When I finally acknowledged them, they then came forward to embrace me and to welcome me.

Even so, you could not say that I was seeing "people." The sensation was more of being in the center of a circle surrounded on all sides by a group of shadowy figures. Also, it was not a finite number that could be counted, just an awareness that whoever was surrounding me was multiple instead of singular. Yet, even though it felt like a group, there was no distinguishable boundary between one entity and the next. There was just this sensation of color leaping out from the background and the feeling that this color surrounding me had a consciousness and an awareness of me in its midst. The nearest analogy in the earth experience I can think of would be the mob of teammates carrying the football quarterback off the playing field on their shoulders after he has just won the championship for the team at the homecoming game. I was being carried and supported by this group of beings, and there was this feeling they were celebrating my existence among their ranks.

In time the group began to be less amorphous and more defined. Then I became aware of three or four individuals who stood out from this group and came into focus even more. While they still did not look like human beings in solid bodies, they were nevertheless beginning to take on some shape and to have individual appearances so that I could distinguish them from each other. They seemed to radiate light from within instead of reflecting light from some outside source. You could almost say they glowed in the dark. But they did not have truly defined boundaries as a human being would. In a way it seemed as though their bodies blended into their surroundings.

After still more time these beings started to take on more humanlike features. That is, in looking at them, I could say they had heads with eyes, a nose, and a mouth. Rather oddly, however, they did not seem to have feet. It was as though these beings were fairly clearly defined from the waist up, but their lower extremities appeared wispy. Moreover, this place did not seem to have a floor or a ground. Everything seemed to rise up out of nothingness. I could see why people had always depicted angels and ghosts as entities in long robes who seemed to just float from one place to another, for that is what these beings appeared to be doing. They reminded me of the three-dimensional holograms I had seen at the science museum. Yet there was nothing at all odd or strange about this. When I was experiencing these phenomena, it seemed completely natural, as though that's exactly the way everything should be.

Once I realized there were beings here, I became even more convinced it was a "real" place I was visiting instead of just a figment of my imagination or the hallucinatory effects of the morphine. These beings had personalities of their own apart from mine. They had thoughts and ideas they could share with me so that I could engage in dialogues instead of feeling I was just playing around in my own mind.

Oddly, no one appeared curious about who I was or what I happened to be doing there. It was as though they knew already. I was not quite sure what their role was with respect to me. They seemed to be watching over me, yet they were very nonintrusive at the same time. By that, I mean no one at any time took the initiative to tell me what to do or where to go. They were extremely passive in that respect. I seemed to be on my own and completely free to do whatever I wanted to do, to come and go as I pleased, to explore all I desired.

I did not stay in this place with these beings for very long at a time. It seemed to me I merely floated into and out of their presence. It was as though there were an unwritten invitation to visit whenever I desired. If I needed comfort, or nurturing, or love, or compassion, or anything at all, these beings were here to accommodate my needs. Satisfied, I would then drift back into the dark passages of my inner world and find myself back in my bed, thinking I had just awakened from a very beautiful dream once more. And then the other realms would fade away into the farthest corners of my inner vision, very soon to be forgotten as the pain and the agony of the cancer came rushing back to become the entire focus of my consciousness.

As time went on and I was coming closer and closer to my death, I was finding it easier to reach these other realms and to believe they were real. It seemed I was becoming better able to sustain my consciousness here and to stay focused here without drifting away. Each time I found the nonphysical realm, I concentrated on keeping it in my focus of attention. And each time I managed to keep it in my focus of attention, it became that much more clear. It was as though I were practicing some skill, that of manipulating my consciousness in a new kind of environment where mental focus and concentration reigned supreme.

I also learned I did not have to do this all alone. The other beings were here to assist me. They were applying their own concentration and mental capabilities to help me sustain my focus and keep me here in their midst. It began to seem like a game of, "Let's see how long she's going to stay here with us *this* time!" I would concentrate for as long as I could, finally slipping away again.

But the next time I came back, I would be welcomed again with cheers: "She's back! Let's see how long she can stay with us *this* time!"

When I could stay focused in this other realm with these beings for extended periods, I was then free to indulge my curiosity. "Where am I? Who are you?" And they would explain I was making a new home for myself, and they were my teachers, guides, and friends, who had come to welcome me home.

When I say they answered my questions, that is misleading. No one "talked" in this place. It was as if I were pondering great mysteries, and then insights were coming right back to me from somewhere within myself. At times I wondered if I might have been asking my own questions and then revealing to myself my own answers from some higher level of my own consciousness.

These beings remained "silent" for the most part, if that is a proper way to describe it. Yet I understood clearly what they were telling me. Their facial expressions told me some things, just as other people's facial expressions communicate their thoughts to us on earth. These beings also radiated different colors in all directions, and those colors began to take on meaning to me. Over time I suppose I was becoming attuned to the communications style here. It was as though all in this place were very psychic, knew they were very psychic, knew everyone else was very psychic, and expected me to be very psychic as well.

The closest analogy I can think of to describe this kind of communication is that which you would have with a dog or cat you have lived with for a long time. It barks or meows and you chatter away unintelligibly, but you each know what the other is thinking. Your vocal expressions are only to attract each other's attention so that you can each listen with your inner ear to what the other is telling you.

Perhaps what I was experiencing in this other realm is similar to what a baby experiences coming into our physical world. Here are all these friendly faces looking in on it, loving it, playing with it, and giving it comfort. They seem to anticipate its every need and to know what it is saying though it is communicating only in cries and coos. Yet at the same time, the baby is learning the spoken language of those around it and absorbing that language into its psyche. Here I was very much like a baby, becoming more aware and learning how to perceive these other realms with my new nonphysical senses. I was absorbing their mental telepathy into my own psyche as a new method of communication.

One of the greatest surprises to me was that I was starting to bring back these

newfound perceptual abilities and senses
when I returned to my physical body. At this
point I was perhaps a month away from "D-
Day." When my family and friends would
come to visit me at my bedside, I began to
notice that they too radiated colors all around
themselves. Some would call this the ability
to see the human aura. Not only did people
have these auras, but also I found everything
else had an aura as well. It was fascinating to
lie there and watch colors streaming off the
walls and rising up from the covers on my
bed. It was as though my bedroom and
everything in it had a consciousness aware of
itself and of me too. Moreover, I began to feel
the presence of my newfound friends from the
nonphysical realms when I was lying in my
bed. I could not "see" them with my physical
eyes, but I knew they were there and I could
communicate with them with the same
mental telepathy I had learned to use in the
nonphysical realms.

By this time too, I was managing to hold on
to the memory of the other realms for longer
periods after I would return to my physical
body. I began to realize I was truly in both the
physical and the nonphysical realms simultaneously.

Sometimes this realization was a bit
disconcerting to me, for I was still somewhat
self-conscious about sharing my experiences
with those around me for fear they would just

discount it all as not "real." I believe what I was experiencing must be very common for people who are ill for a long time before they die. I believe they are exploring the nonphysical realms while they are waiting to die, just as I was. And I suspect most of them do not dare speak of their experiences for the same reasons I had: They fear they will be thought to be just imagining things and to be hallucinating. It's unfortunate that this should be so, for if the dying were encouraged to talk more about their experiences, the rest of humanity would see there truly is a life beyond death and would not be as afraid to die themselves.

I suppose I was lucky, for I had a few people around me who were open-minded and who were understanding of my need to talk about what was happening to me. Their curiosity encouraged me to share with them what I was experiencing in the other realms and to feel that my experiences were valid.

All the way up to the day I died, although the greater part of my consciousness was by that time off cavorting in other realms, I was still very much aware of the presence of my friends and loved ones who came to visit me at my bedside. Even though it seemed to them that I was unconscious or asleep, I felt their love and received it. It is very important for you to know that, though dying persons may appear to be asleep, in a coma, or under the influence of strong narcotics, they can still feel your presence and receive your love and concern. Just sitting there with a dying person is all that's needed. Or, at that point, you don't even have to be in the same room with them. You only need to think about them and to feel loving thoughts toward them, and they will most certainly receive your thoughts and feelings, just as I did.

Each time I made the crossing into the other realms, I gained more courage to explore them even further. And in exploring them often over time, I began to feel comfortable in the nonphysical realms. As my cancer took its toll, I found myself staying over on the other side of the veil separating the dimensions, while I was spending less and less time in my physical body. When I was fully confident I could sustain my focus and maintain my consciousness in my new environment, I began to feel I could finally let go of my physical life and bring my consciousness home to the nonphysical realms for good.

Chapter Three

Pulling the Plug

The decision to die is a serious decision, to say the least. What made it so serious for me was that the decision was entirely mine to make. Knowing the decision at this point would be final and irrevocable, I took my good old time to make up my mind whether, at last, I should pull the plug on my physical body and allow the cancer to do me in.

Little did I realize, however, how difficult it would be to pull the plug on my life as Susan Wells. It seemed the cancer was making me extremely miserable, but it wasn't killing me.

My body hung in there and resisted the onslaught of cancer cells. Each time I was examined by the doctors and nurses, they shook their heads and wondered why I was still alive. They kept giving me more morphine to control the pain, but my body was resisting it and becoming immune to the larger doses they were giving me.

Ironically, a part of my consciousness was ensconced in my ailing body begging to be released from the pain and misery of my cancer; another part was keeping my body alive from the nonphysical realm where I knew only joy and peace and felt no pain at all. One part of me was holding on to the pain and misery; the other part was struggling to get rid of it.

I was in a quandary because I was trying to "have my cake and eat it too." Had I truly accomplished everything I had set out to do? Were there any loose ends left over that I would regret not having tied up while I still had the chance? Was I truly ready to let go of my life as Susan Wells?

Finally, I reached a point where it seemed useless to keep my body alive any longer because it was rapidly losing its function anyway. Thus, about a week before I pulled out, I started the final shutdown. I asked for help from my newfound friends, guides, and teachers in the nonphysical realms, for I was afraid I was never going to make it across the threshold on my own. In essence, what we did was to combine our consciousness and willpower to focus on the cancer cells so that they would grow even faster. We then focused on the various body systems to make my body break down and shut down for good.

The biggest astonishment about my death was how detached I was from my physical body by the time I reached the last week or two of my life on earth. From the physical standpoint I looked mighty sick indeed as my body started breaking down. It frightened my family to see me lose all control over my digestive and kidney functions and to see me hemorrhaging from my nose and mouth as I was shutting down my lungs. To hear my family speak of it, I was in excruciating pain, suffering terribly, and engaging in a humongous battle with my body.

But from my perspective, I was not much aware of the suffering my body was going through. I was here in the peace, warmth, and joy of the nonphysical realms, cut off and isolated from the trauma my body was feeling at that point. My consciousness was by this time focused almost entirely in this new home I had created for myself in the afterlife. So while my body was writhing in agony, my "real" self was laughing and dancing and jumping for joy.

The people who suffer the most are the family members who are sitting around the bedside watching the dying person, for they see how dramatic the breakdown is, and they imagine it must be very painful. They also hear the dying person moaning and groaning, sometimes gasping in agony. They think she must be in great distress. The loved ones see the suffering of the physical body and think the *person* is suffering. And so they feel sorry for their beloved one who must lie there and suffer like that. But all that apparent suffering is just the physical body going through its own process, while the dying person's conscious awareness is somewhere else. In truth, the dying person is off romping in meadows, having a grand party with her friends in the nonphysical realms who are celebrating her homecoming to the afterlife.

I'm told my experience was not unique. The spiritual essence of most people withdraws its focus from the physical body when the pain becomes too tough to bear. Of course, for cancer and other painful diseases, there are also medical assistance and powerful drugs to squelch the pain and relieve the suffering. But the primary factor is that the consciousness is focused elsewhere.

A similar process occurs in people who die suddenly, as in an automobile accident or on a battlefield. Their inner consciousness knows what is about to happen and they pull out just before the impact. After all, who wants to hurt and suffer if they don't have to?

Human consciousness is wonderful in that respect, for it knows when to get in there and feel and it knows when to get out of there and detach.

The same phenomenon occurs at the other end of physical life too. From a physical standpoint, the baby's arrival into the world through the birth canal is no picnic either. But it is the mother bringing the baby into the world who suffers the most from the baby's birth. The baby's consciousness is still for the most part focused in the nonphysical world and comes into the physical world only after the pain and suffering of its newborn physical body are behind it.

Even after I made the decision to pull the plug on my physical life, it would still take several more days for my body to shut down completely. I knew what I was up against even before I pulled the plug because, by the time I reached "D-Day," I was already becoming quite savvy with the manipulation of time and space in the nonphysical realms. Thus my deathbed scene and ultimate demise may have been playing themselves out in a linear fashion in the physical realm, but in the nonphysical realms I was already in the ever-present "now" playing with the idea of time moving in all different directions at once. For all practical purposes, I was dead already, but my body did not realize it.

Finally, on the last day, starting about twelve hours before the end, I came back for one last ditch effort to pull loose from my physical body and to let go of my lifetime as Susan Wells.

There is a great deal written about the last few hours or minutes of the dying process, and I have the impression each person's experience is unique. In all cases, however, the consciousness (or the spirit, or the soul, if you prefer) pulls out of the body. Sometimes the body trembles for just a moment as the consciousness rushes out. Other times it's as though somebody has poked a hole in the body and the consciousness escapes out the hole.

Little did I realize what a struggle it would be to release my own consciousness from my physical body. The process, I had been told, was supposed to be very simple. First, I was to focus on gathering up my consciousness. Then I was supposed to pull it out of my body, starting with my feet and moving up toward my head. But my consciousness seemed to stick to the inside of my body like glue. It was terribly frustrating, to say the least. Here I was, literally yanking and pulling myself out of my body, but "myself" was still holding on for dear life and would not come loose. What a dilemma! For several hours I had a tug of war with my body. The harder I struggled to pull loose, the tighter my body seemed to hold on to me. I was getting exhausted by the struggle. And so were my loved ones who were standing by witnessing it.

From my perspective at this point, I then found myself in two places at once. A part of me was in my body struggling to get free and another part of me went off to the nonphysical realms to call my teachers and friends for help. They came forward and gathered around me, giving me the courage and strength I needed, coaching me and cheering me on.

It all began then to feel as though I were playing a role in a drama, like a mother in a labor room undergoing a very difficult delivery. All the doctors and nurses are coaching her and encouraging her on. She wants the struggle to be over with because she is exhausted. She does not know how much longer she can go on like this. But they are telling her to keep pushing, to not give up, to keep trying, to keep breathing, to keep pushing. In my case, my guides and coaches were not telling me to push, but to *pull*.

Finally, I gave it one last heroic effort and pulled with all my might. All of a sudden I heard this sound—something like fabric tearing, or perhaps the sound you hear when you are pulling Velcro apart. My consciousness came loose from the inside of my legs and pulled right on out of my body.

The last thing I remember thinking as I was moving out through the top of my head was, "At last! It's over! I did it! I'm free at last, free at last, thank God Almighty, I'm free at last!" I planted a smile on my physical face, turned around to take one last look at myself lying in my bed, said farewell to my family, and backed away from the scene at my deathbed.

It then felt as though I were moving backward through a tunnel. The scene in my bedroom, which had until that moment taken up my entire field of vision, shrank down to a tiny circle, and then to a dot, before it disappeared entirely as I soared higher and higher away. Then everything became very loud for a moment and I started to hear a rushing sound, as though I were accelerating in speed and were taking off like a rocket ship into outer space.

It seemed dark at first, but then I noticed a light that started getting brighter and brighter until it was a brilliant white. In addition to white, it seemed to radiate every other color imaginable. I suddenly realized what they had meant when they said white was the combination of all the other colors. Spread out before me were hundreds, thousands, millions, *gazillions* of colors; yet they were all converging into this brilliant white light.

I would have thought light that bright would hurt and would cause me to flinch from its brightness. But I didn't flinch at all.

It was as though the light couldn't possibly get too bright. The brighter it became, the more joy and ecstasy I felt. But at the same time I felt as though I had the capacity to feel even more light and more ecstasy. I had a glimpse of what it must feel like to be God, for in that moment I felt I had merged with God. It finally occurred to me what they had meant when they said you go back to the Light when you die. Comparatively speaking, I had been in darkness, and my physical body had felt heavy and oppressive. But then I took this wave out that could best be described as a crescendo into infinity.

When I got back to the nonphysical realms from having pulled the plug on my physical body, I found myself with a large group of beings who surrounded me and cheered at my homecoming. I felt once more like the quarterback who had carried his team to victory and was being hauled off the field on the shoulders of his teammates. It seemed as though all heaven was celebrating.

Chapter Four

Final Examination
and Graduation

*O*nce I had pulled the plug for good on my physical body, it was time for me to finish the transition stage of my death and rebirth. In other words, I needed to do some additional work to let go of my life as Susan Wells before I could go on with my adventures here in the afterlife. This phase of my development could perhaps be described as an incubation period.

First, my teachers and guides sat me down and told me about what I would be going through, answering all my questions about it.

They also gave me a choice as to whether or not I wanted to go through with it. I don't know what would have happened if I had said, "No." Perhaps there would have been an alternate route for me to take. Perhaps they would have left me in the state of consciousness I was in until I tired of it and decided to move forward. I suspect this latter is what would have happened, for they assured me it was my choice and I could determine when I was ready for it. Needless to say, I felt apprehensive about it.

As soon as I agreed to go through with the incubation, plans and preparations were made for the anticipated event. I had been told it would feel as if I were going to sleep and dreaming. Then at some later time I would wake up again and probably would have little actual memory of what had taken place. I was also told the reason they were calling this an "incubation" was that I would be placed into a bed, and the bed would be inserted into a chamber, similar to an incubator babies on earth are kept in until they reach a stage of growth and development at which they can sustain life on their own.

The purpose of the incubation, I was told, was to clear out any memories of my just-completed earth life that no longer would serve me in my new life and that might hold me back from the optimum evolution of my soul. They used the analogy of taking a rough cut diamond and polishing off all its rough edges, then cutting the facets into it so that it would reflect the greatest amount of light possible, allowing its full beauty to come out. These "rough edges" were primarily old attitudes and beliefs I had brought with me from my earth life that needed to be discarded. Among the most pertinent of these was the idea of right and wrong, or good and evil.

In the process of this incubation, I would also be bringing out any remaining shadows from my life, from things I regretted doing, to events I wished had not happened, to situations that had made me feel guilt or shame. All of these were to be brought to the surface and scraped away so that my true light could shine through.

You will realize human consciousness, especially in babies and small children, has a wonderful capacity to fly away whenever anything distressing occurs. Psychologists call this dissociation. The spiritual or soul essence of the person brings these experiences into conscious awareness much later in adulthood, if at all, when such memories can be handled. Sometimes human memories are left buried in the unconscious mind for an entire lifetime, never to be revealed until the spirit leaves the body once more and comes back into the afterlife.

Once safely back home again, we then can examine our lifetime as a human being and can bring up *all* the memories of what we did and what happened to us. We can then heal from our experiences and learn the lessons they offered us. We do this life review after we are completely into this realm; that is, after we have "died."

In this realm our memory is much more clear than yours. I don't know quite why that is. I do know I can remember much more of my life as Susan Wells, and what I remember is much more detailed. There is not the forgetting or the distortion of memory with which you are so often plagued. I'm told it is because memory is just a tuning in on a certain vibratory frequency. Once we are tuned in, it is as though the original event is here and now and we can live it all again just as we experienced it the first time. Not only that, but we can tune in on all the various attributes of a memory, such as the associated sights, sounds, smells, feelings and sensations. This is true even if we were not necessarily aware of those attributes when we were first experiencing the remembered event.

For example, we might have been somewhere standing on a street corner waiting for a friend to meet us. We might have been so focused on the people passing by that we did not hear a plane fly overhead.

When we now tune in on the remembered event, we will be aware of everything that occurred, even the plane that we were not aware of originally.

It is much easier to see all the aspects of every event from this perspective. For example, we might have been embroiled in an emotional turmoil during some event, and we could not see all the factors that may have led up to or have arisen out of that event. From my current perspective I can now go back and review every event in my lifetime as Susan Wells, even the most mundane events from my childhood I had long since forgotten when I was in my later adult years.

I can tune in, for instance, on a summer afternoon when I was a small baby lying in my crib, and the event will come into focus as though it is now happening. I can also see all the events leading up to that particular afternoon, and I can see all the probable events leading away from the event I now have in focus.

I now realize my lifetime as Susan Wells was only one of literally hundreds of lifetimes that were "Susan Wells." At each crossroad I came to in my life I thought I was making a choice and then taking one of the roads. But, in fact, a part of my consciousness actually spun off and took each of the other roads as well. I can now go back and see what happened to each of the other Susan Wellses who took the other paths I did not take. All of this is extremely fascinating to me, not only because it is showing me my life was much more rich and full than I suspected, but also because it gives me greater understanding now of the choices I did make and why I took the paths I took. Even more important, it shows me no particular path I took was necessarily good or bad. I have come to realize, in the overall scheme, because this larger aspect of myself took all the possible paths that could be taken, the paths were all equally valuable and in perfect balance.

In preparation for this incubation period, I spent a great deal of time in what you might call "therapy" sessions with my teachers. We sat down together and reviewed my life from beginning to end and talked about all the events that had happened about which I still felt concern or still had judgments. I then worked on forgiving myself and coming to the realization that everything I had done and everything that had happened to me had a purpose. This purpose was simply my learning and growth.

I also learned some things I had done to others that I later regretted had actually been planned by me before my birth. In other words, those people needed to have experiences for their own growth that, in our human eyes, would look as though they were being victimized. In order to have those experiences, someone needed to volunteer to participate with the victim. I learned there was no right or wrong in my actions. I was merely playing a role in a drama others were creating for themselves. This was somewhat difficult for me to comprehend, as you could well imagine, since schools, churches, and governments had spent my entire lifetime filling me full of beliefs that certain activities were "right" and certain other activities were "wrong."

My new teachers in the spirit realms kept telling me over and over again that right and wrong, good and evil, and other such ethical concepts were useful only in the human mind. They were no longer useful in the afterlife and could even become a hindrance to my further spiritual growth.

The teachers who acted as my therapists were very compassionate. They showed me my life was perfect just as it was, and everybody who is human does some things about which they later feel guilt or shame. My teachers had no judgment whatsoever about anything I had done. Instead, when I felt especially shameful about something, they showed me what they had done in their own past lifetimes that seemed even worse.

As I already said, the purpose of all this therapy was to bring me to a point where I could take away all judgment about myself, where I could forgive myself and see every event as a beautiful piece in the wonderful jigsaw of life. Thus the therapy sessions with my teachers were enlightening and healing experiences for me.

Human beings are always concerned with the questions: "Am I on the right path?" "Did I do the right thing?" The answers are, "Yes, you are," and, "Yes, you did." For I have learned it truly doesn't matter what path you choose to take. Each path has a gift of learning and enlightenment to present to you. It truly doesn't matter if you do one thing as opposed to another. Each thing you do is perfect in and of itself.

Once I had come to accept my entire life and every event in it as perfect just the way it was, I was then ready to go into the incubation chamber to remove all the scars, blemishes, and dark spots in my psyche.

The length of time this process takes depends on the person going through it. Although we don't have "time" as you know it, I understand it can occur in a matter of seconds or extend for thousands of years in your time frame. The process seems to be shortened for those who were well aware of their spiritual roots in their earth lives and had done much of the review and recovery work before they made the transition out of their physical bodies. For others the process is extended if they were cut off from their spirituality or if they had rigid religious beliefs that left them wounded and scarred with unnecessary guilt or self blame.

There are even some who, because of their religious beliefs, may go into a coma-like state and float around in suspended animation for thousands of years, as you understand time, because they are waiting for some "savior" to come along and "raise them from the dead." For those unfortunate beings, there are rescue teams who work with them and try to make them realize no one is going to "save" them except themselves. Thus, for some, there may be an enormous amount of work involved just to bring them into this realm before their teachers can begin to work with them to help them through the incubation process.

As for myself, I seemed to sail right through the process because I had dedicated my life to my spiritual growth, first through organized religious structures, and then onward and upward on my own spiritual path beyond organized religion. I had also worked on my spiritual growth through various twelve-step programs, which taught me to turn my unmanageable problems over to my Higher Power, as I understood that concept. Finally, when I was making the transition into these realms in fits and starts during my long bout with cancer, I came to know and trust the beings working with me as my teachers and guides who were leading me to my highest growth.

You might say I came into the afterlife champing at the bit, ready to move forward on my spiritual quest and willing to do anything to make that growth as speedy as possible. Thus my incubation period was comparatively "short." But I want to point out there is no right or wrong in either a short or a long incubation period. They don't give out grades here, and there is no such thing as competition here.

The actual period of "time" I spent in the incubation chamber itself is unknown, for my consciousness was at that point being broken down and reformulated. The process was somewhat analogous to what a larva must experience in a cocoon. As I understand it, the larva's entire physical structure and chemistry breaks down, and then it is built back up from ground zero to emerge from the cocoon as a beautiful butterfly. In my incubation "cocoon" my physical consciousness was torn down to its basic elements and built back up again as a nonphysical consciousness, whereupon I emerged as a brand new being.

Whereas the larva goes into the cocoon with one body and set of skills (crawling on many feet) and emerges with a completely different body and set of skills (flying through the air), I too emerged from my incubation period as a being who had a new body and a new set of skills. But just as the butterfly must adapt itself to its new body and learn how to fly, I too had to learn how to manipulate my new body after I emerged from the incubation chamber.

There is a saying on earth that you are born alone and you die alone. The same feeling prevails in this realm. We move through a process of going within our own selves as we get ready to cross over the threshold from earth to this realm. We then stay in our inner space for as long as necessary to reconnect with the source of our being or, as some of you would call it, with our Creator.

Looking back on it, I now realize my entire bout with cancer, my death, my incubation period, and my rebirth in the afterlife was one transaction that pulled me out of one world, drew me back to the source of my being, and brought me forth once more as a brand new being in a brand new world.

PART II

OTHER PERSPECTIVES
ON DEATH

Chapter Five

Surprise! You're Dead!!

There are tens of thousands of human beings who transfer off the face of the earth each day, but they don't all come to the same place I did. They pass out of their bodies at various levels of the stream of consciousness, depending on their beliefs.

Some people stay closely bound to their earth life and actually hang around their old neighborhoods. You don't realize they are there because they no longer have physical bodies you can see. Nevertheless, they are still wandering around and they can see you.

Others try to move as far away from physical life as they can, as though the experience of human beingness were some sort of disease from which they are trying to recover. Still others who come into these realms are so disoriented by the new rules of nonphysicality that their teachers and guardians must put them into institutions much like your convalescent homes. They can then go to sleep and be gradually awakened and given therapy to help them become oriented. After all, you can imagine how frightening it can seem to people who always believed in only physical existence and adamantly disbelieved in anything they could not see, touch, or taste to suddenly find themselves in a place where they can walk through walls and flash in and out of their surroundings as quickly as their minds can flit from one thought to another.

I, for one, was introduced to the afterlife while still ensconced in a body, and I traveled here a great deal while I was battling my cancer. That is one of the advantages of a lengthy final illness. People can come here to explore and get used to this place from their deathbed so that it will not be such a shock to the senses when they finally pass over to the afterlife for good. Others, for whatever reason, will find themselves here and may not even realize they are "dead." They may believe they are just having a bad dream, the kind they might have from eating too much pizza just before going to bed.

There are many situations in which they could die so suddenly that they wouldn't even realize they were dying. For example, they could be having some surgery and be under the influence of an anesthetic when something unexpected occurs. Perhaps they have a bad reaction to the anesthetic or there is some other glitch in their bodily functions. Let's say, for instance, their heart stops and the doctors cannot make it start beating again. They might be completely unaware their time is up and they are about to die.

Even though they always know at their soul level when their life is coming to an end—and they do have a choice in the matter—this choice is often made at other levels of their consciousness. Perhaps they have been making the decision in their sleep state and they don't remember it. Perhaps they have made the decision in their unconscious mind. Nevertheless, the decision has been made and they agreed to it, whether they realize it or not.

Now they're in the operating room and the situation presents a wonderful opportunity to pull the plug on their physical life. What happens next depends on their belief about "death." Let's say they do not believe in an afterlife. So now they die on the operating table and the doctors cannot bring them back to life. What happens next?

They may find themselves doing what they believe would have been the next logical step. For example, if they went under the anesthesia knowing they were undergoing surgery, they might come to awareness in a bed in a recovery room or in a medical ward. They may even lie there for a long time thinking they have just awakened from the operation.

But then they may become aware that there is something wrong. They might see nurses and doctors coming in and out of the room but not paying attention to them. They might ask, "Why are all these nurses ignoring me? They act as if I'm not even here. Don't they realize how much pain I'm in right after my surgery?" And then they might suddenly realize, "Hey, wait a minute! I'm *not* in any pain! I just came through an operation and I don't feel a thing. What's going on here?" They might become truly anxious and confused at this point and may even want to get up and go find a nurse or a doctor to find out what's going on.

This might bring on the next clue. As they get up to move around, they may realize they can move with no effort whatsoever. They may even feel almost weightless. The room might start to catch their attention as well:

"Hey, wait a minute! These walls look almost as though I could walk right through them!"

Or they might be in their room and start thinking they can find someone at the nurse's station to help them and, all of a sudden, they will be standing at the nurse's station and not know how they got there. By this point they may begin to believe they are dreaming. After all, you don't just disappear from one scene and reappear in another scene except in your dreams.

But then the situation may become even more bizarre. They might start moving down the hospital corridor and see a number of doctors and nurses coming toward them. But instead of seeing them and acknowledging them, the doctors and nurses might look right through them. The doctors and nurses may even walk right through them and keep on going. Can you imagine what you might start thinking about your sanity if you are standing somewhere and someone comes right up to you, walks right through you, and keeps on going without so much as a "Howdy do"?

At this point most people will throw their hands up in exasperation and shout, "Will somebody please tell me what's going on here?" And of course, as it always is in the nonphysical realms, as soon as the question is asked, someone will immediately appear with an answer. In more technical terms, the asking of the question will send out a wave of energy that will be broadcast everywhere at once, and the entity who has the answer for that particular question will hear it and respond to it.

Most likely, the entity with the answer will be a teacher or a guide assigned to help the recently deceased through their death process. Even more likely, the teacher or guide will have been waiting around for them to ask for help. Until that time teachers and guides know not to interfere with the process. But as soon as a plea for help (or a query, or even the slightest hint) comes flowing out of someone's consciousness, all heaven breaks loose (to paraphrase a popular expression), and help is on the way. The teachers and guides will rush forward to assist the deceased through their confusion and explain what has happened. The teachers and guides will answer their questions and show them what they need to do next.

When death comes as a total surprise like this, you can imagine that anybody going through this experience will be quite shocked at the news. They will react the same as I reacted when my doctor told me my cancer was back and this time it wasn't going to go away. The first reaction is denial: "Oh, no!! I can't believe it! You're kidding, aren't you? Tell me it isn't so!"

In my case, I still had my physical life when I was told the news. Those who have been found wandering around in the hallways of the "after-death" hospital don't have that shock absorber. To them the news is even more shocking. But oftentimes the words that come out of their mouth will be exactly the same: "Oh, no!! I can't believe it! You're kidding, aren't you? Tell me it isn't so!" Only, in this instance, they might also add, "You mean I'm *dead*?"

Once they get over the shock of their demise, then they will have many questions to ask about their situation. On the other hand, the news might be so shocking that it may make them faint, for there are some people whose psyche cannot take such news. They may even sink into a state of consciousness similar to a coma and stay in suspended animation until the idea sinks in and they can accept it.

I am told there are some here who are so shocked by the news of their "death" that they go into a "coma" for thousands of years. But, of course, the amount of time they remain in this state does not matter, for we do not have a linear concept of time here. Eventually, however, they will reawaken once more and will gradually be pulled out of their shock and disbelief.

Chapter Six

Even Bigger Surprise!
You're _Not_ Dead!!

We all know many human beings who do not believe in life beyond the death of the physical body. For them the concept of a nonphysical reality is a shock. Just put yourself into their mind for a moment and imagine how they must feel when they first encounter the afterlife. If you believed your death was the end of your existence, and then you died, and everything did not go black and silent as you had expected, wouldn't you be shocked? If you found yourself in motion and suddenly started seeing colors, flashing lights, and all sorts of objects you could not comprehend flying all around you, wouldn't you be alarmed? You would wonder if perhaps you had not died but instead had gone insane.

Such a situation could throw you into a panic in a very short time. Being in a panic, you would find your outer world suddenly moving faster and faster, and you would find yourself tumbling and falling, spinning around, slipping and sliding. That is precisely the experience of some who leave their earth bodies behind.

Another common experience of those who believe death is the end of their existence is for everything to black out on them, just as they always believed it would. To them it might feel like a solid sleep state. Nothing. Total darkness. Never-ending blackness. And they might stay that way for a long, long time, maybe even for years, as you measure time.

At some point, though, they will begin to realize they are still aware. There is nothing going on. Everything is pitch black. Everything is completely silent. But maybe they are not dead after all because, if they were truly dead, they would not be aware of the darkness and the silence.

This flash of insight will then open them up to a new thought: "If I'm aware, then I must still be alive. Death must not be the end of it all. There must be more. Otherwise, why would I still be here thinking these things?" With that thought, they might start to think some more. "If it's black and it's silent, perhaps it's because I'm believing that. Maybe I'm just floating around here with my eyes and ears closed."

They might then begin to notice something in their field of vision. Perhaps they'll see a flash of light. Perhaps the pitch blackness won't be as black anymore but will start to turn into various shades of gray. Perhaps they will hear some music or a whoosh of wind. And then they might notice other colors creeping into the scene, as though they are now floating around in animated suspension. And then other visions might flash into their mind. At this point they will begin to realize they still have a mind and they are still conscious.

For many, this is a staggering notion because some scientists have said your mind and your consciousness are all a product of your brain chemistry. Can you imagine one of these beings, who believed those scientists, and who believed their mind and consciousness were left to molder in the grave with their decaying body, suddenly coming to the realization that their mind, their awareness, and their consciousness have survived?

As soon as they come to this realization, they are on their way to waking up and coming back to life in a new realm. Once they realize they still have their mind, they will begin to play with thoughts and ideas. These thoughts and ideas will then quickly manifest into scenery and events, just as your thoughts and ideas manifest into scenery and events in your dream world.

Once these beings start thinking again, start seeing things, and start experiencing things happening, they will begin to wonder if there is anybody else here with them. After all, we human beings are social beings. We have been used to having other human beings (not to mention animals, plants, and a myriad of other life forms) around us every moment of our lives. These beings will soon get the idea that, if they are still aware, they must still be alive. If they are still alive, then everyone else who dies must still be alive as well. And if that is true, then where are they?

No sooner than they ask the question, other beings will appear. In keeping with their human tendency to mingle with others and to communicate with them, they will reach out and ask those other beings, "Who are you? Where am I? What is this place? What happened? Do you know what's going on here?" And the other beings who have the answers to those questions will let our dear little lost and confused friends know that they are alive, that they have left their physical bodies behind, but that does not mean they are *dead.* No sireee, Bob!

One thing I am truly thankful for: I opened up to my spiritual nature while I was still in a physical body. I have seen people arrive in this realm who thought death was the end of life. Many of them were quite confused when they arrived here and found out they truly did not die, nor will they ever. They believed one thing but got another, and they doubted their sanity as a result.

Of course, there are teachers and guides who will work with these people to let them know that, no, they are not crazy. But it is quite a shock to the psyche nonetheless. For one thing, these people sometimes won't believe what the teachers and guides are telling them. They think they are in some halfway place waiting to *really* die. It's as though they think whatever it was that killed them didn't work, and now they have to go through the death process all over again until they really do die.

I can't stress enough how important it is to believe in an afterlife, for if you don't and you live on after your death anyway, you can be quite taken apart by the news that you're still alive.

Chapter Seven

Suicide and Euthanasia

What about suicide and other forms of assisted death? On the one hand, you could say every death is a suicide, for we each choose to die. Death is never an involuntary act, no matter how it may seem. It doesn't matter whether the form of death is a murder, an execution, an accident, a result of war, plague, or otherwise. All deaths and their time, manner, and place have been determined long before the actual event. It is only from the human perspective, with its mass belief that all events in life are accidental, that death should somehow be accidental as well.

The reaction of humankind to the news of one's death or impending death as a great tragedy is just that: a reaction. Death is no tragedy, no matter what the circumstances. It is always an opportunity. It affords a transition into other realms where further living goes on and where there is more possibility to grow and to learn.

You would wonder then, why not just push it along here and choose some other form of death that might be more gentle? Yes, that's it! Let's all have a kinder, gentler death. Instead of lingering around for months and months in excruciating pain watching your body being eaten alive with cancer, why not just take a gun to your head? Instead of taking a bullet in your head from a murderer's gun, why not have a stroke, slip into a coma, and die before the bullet reaches its target? Instead of getting all smashed up and squished to death in a three-car pile up, why not just take an injection that puts you to sleep like the euthanasia your veterinarian performs on your dog? Instead of lying in a hospital emergency room with your heart-stabbing pain, the doctors slapping those paddles on your chest and shooting electricity through your body to start your heart beating again, why not just blow yourself up on a land mine on a battlefield? Boom! You're dead before you even know what hit you.

You see, it probably doesn't matter which form of death you choose. They all have their advantages and disadvantages. You might feel sorry for the murder victim ("Oh, but his life was cut short by someone else just when he had everything to live for.") Perhaps the murder victim might have wished he could linger around in a sick bed for a while to get used to the idea of dying, tasting it slowly over a period of months.

So why not euthanasia? Or some other form of assisted death? You know how I was begging to be put out of my misery in those last few months before my own "D-Day." It was all I could do to keep from getting on the phone to Dr. Kevorkian. If only he would jump on the next plane to California to put me out of my misery. If only he hadn't been busy defending himself in a courtroom in Michigan at the time. Those of you who witnessed my demise knew I was one of the great proponents of assisted suicide or euthanasia when I was going through my own suffering.

But looking back on it now from my present perspective, I'm glad you did not take me up on it. For as I was begging to die with one part of my consciousness, there was another greater part of my consciousness that was orchestrating my entire bout with the cancer and stretching it out as long as possible. I could not perceive that orchestration through my physical pain. All I could perceive, in fact, was my physical pain, and I wondered why I had to suffer that much. But now from my present perspective, I see that my suffering was very necessary. I realize now I had planned a long and painful demise because I wanted to experience it that way. I wanted to know what pain was in all its aspects. I wanted to experience it inside and outside. I wanted it to take over and become the entire focus of my awareness. For in the pain came a new level of consciousness I was striving to reach. It provided a mechanism for me to learn how to focus my attention solidly and unwaveringly on a single event. It enhanced my ability to concentrate. As the pain took over, I saw my consciousness stand up to that pain as two warriors stand up to each other in battle, each one holding firm to his resolve, neither one flinching. I saw my courage grow with each passing day as I faced the pain and became one with it.

It has been said that there is not much difference between extreme pain and extreme pleasure. Having been through the most extreme pain imaginable, I can attest to the truth of that statement.

The point is that my bout with cancer brought me growth and enlightenment. Having been through the relentless pain and suffering, in the end, I learned to become one with it, to embrace it, to respect it, if not even to love it. And having been through such an intense experience, there is not much that could topple me at this point. Yes, it is a horrible way to die, and, like the California bar examination, it is not something anybody would want to do twice. But in the end I survived and moved on through it, and I have grown in my awareness because of it.

We started out asking whether suicide or assisted suicide is a proper way to die. And after my long diatribe on the virtues of pain and suffering, I bet you think I'm going to take the martyr's stance and say you should never bump yourself off by your own means. But I won't. In spite of what churches say about suicide being some great mortal sin for which you will be cast into the hellish fires forever, I say you have nothing to worry about on that score.

There are some I have met here who have committed suicide and have regretted it afterwards because they realized they did not complete everything they set out to do in that particular lifetime. Now they want to go back and live another lifetime to finish up old business. But there are others who see their suicide as the very thing that saved them. They found themselves on a downward spiral from which they saw no other escape. So instead of to keep spiraling downward and to have to dig themselves out of a deep mess they had made of their life, they saw suicide as a way to cut their losses and to get back onto their chosen path more quickly.

There are some who say you shouldn't cut your losses, that if you have made a mess, you should live with the consequences. Those are the same people who see the filing of bankruptcy as a personal failure, instead of the fresh start the law intended it to be. But in the end, it does not matter what anyone else says or thinks about it—not churches, not governments, not neighbors. The only one who matters is you. What do *you* believe? Deep down in your gut, in that quiet place only you can reach inside of you, what is that still small voice saying to *you*? No matter what it tells you—"Yes, go for it!" or "No, don't you dare!" or "Well, why don't you wait and see what happens tomorrow?"—realize your own inner voice knows the truth and trust its guidance.

It was this small inner voice that kept whispering to me that I learned to listen to and to trust. This inner voice told me to wait and see what would happen tomorrow. And tomorrow. And tomorrow. And tomorrow. I learned to take each day one day at a time until, one day, I woke up and I had no more pain. I was bathing in the light of God-All-That-Is, feeling love, compassion, and healing wash all the memory of pain away and replacing it with an ecstasy I never could have imagined in my wildest dreams. At that point, the issue of suicide, or assisted suicide, or euthanasia—call it what you will—was moot.

Chapter Eight

Birds Do It. Trees Do It.

For every physical life form in the earth realm there is a nonphysical counterpart. Animals and plants leave the earth under similar circumstances as do we human beings. That is, they "die" and then they transfer their consciousness here. And just as we human beings have an incubation period in which we shed our physicality, so do animals and plants. As you can imagine, the transition is much the same.

In some ways animals and plants have an easier time of "dying" than do we human beings. For one thing, they don't have the rational logic and intellectual reasoning powers that human beings have. They therefore don't talk themselves out of what they can feel with their inner knowing. They instinctively know the source of their being. They have an intuitive knowing that they have created themselves on earth in order to explore physical living conditions.

A tree soul, for example, is exploring all aspects of tree-ness, both nonphysical and physical. When it sends a portion of its consciousness into the physical realm of earth, a tree is doing so in order to learn what it feels like to grow tall and straight, to spread its limbs upward and outward, to create a canopy of leaves in which to feel the kiss of the sun and the wonderful wet tickling of the rain drops. It explores the concept of growing and of just "being," instead of "doing." It learns to live in cycles of night and day, of summer and winter, of active growth and dormancy. It learns to perceive other trees, plants, animals, insects, and, of course, human beings, sensing all these various life forms as different frequencies of energy. It faces challenges to its health from diseases, fires, and assaults by chain saws. And, above all, it learns patience. If you took half a century to develop from a tiny seed to a full grown specimen, and then could stretch out your lifetime for perhaps several centuries longer, you too would learn patience.

Even in the face of "danger" to its life, a tree knows it is more than its physical body. Thus when a tree leaves the physical realm and comes here, it comes with a wisdom not often seen in human beings. Moreover, just as we human beings set ourselves free from the constraints of physical bodies and release ourselves from the laws of time and space when we arrive here in the nonphysical realms, so do trees. Thus they enjoy the freedom to move around, to twist and bend to their heart's content, to dance and sing, if they so desire. And they enjoy blending with other consciousness, as well, so that they may gain knowledge of what it is like to be a bird, or a snake, or a human being. They love to blend with the rain so that they may slither down the leaves and bark of other trees, to know what it feels like to be the giver of the wet tickle as well as the receiver.

Animals too have their stories to tell about their lifetimes on earth. All in all, they see the earth as a wonderful playground to romp and run, to hunt and explore, to enjoy the physical pleasures of eating, sleeping, and bearing offspring. And even though they face the frustrations of being predators outsmarted by wily prey and the fright of vulnerable prey being outrun by predators, they don't see either of these situations as the "tragedies" and "disasters" we human beings seem to perceive about everything in our lives.

In fact, the animals find our unhappiness and feelings of guilt and shame, not to mention our obsessive-compulsive behaviors in general, to be incomprehensible. They wonder if human beings—who sit around their television sets watching news of violence and dramas of people mistreating other people in every conceivable fashion—are some form of genetic mutation. They wonder about our sanity when we judge our self-worth by impossible notions of beauty, when we spend our lives starving ourselves in order to "look" thin, when we kill others of our own species because they have different beliefs or look different from ourselves. And they cannot understand at all our battle of the sexes wherein males don't understand females and females don't understand males. "What's to understand?" they query.

I'm sure most human beings have no idea that animals and plants would even be aware of us and all our foibles. But they are. It was truly amazing to me to find out that plants and animals know a lot more about us than we know about them. They find it incomprehensible that we should consider them to be below us on our evolutionary scale. And they smile knowingly (or the plant/animal equivalent thereof) when we assume they have no conscious awareness. Truly it would seem they would have the last laugh when we all meet again here in the nonphysical realms. But laugh they do not, or at least not *at* us, for I have also found plants and animals to be lacking completely in such judgmental attitudes.

While they are living with us on earth, our pet dogs and cats spend a great deal of their time sleeping. Out of any twenty-four hour day, they may be sleeping for eighteen to twenty of those hours, depending on how much they are distracted by activities that keep them awake. Have you ever wondered why they sleep that much? The reason is that they are then reconnecting with the nonphysical portion of their consciousness residing in other dimensions. They often come here and wander around in the nonphysical realms, where they participate as pets of others who knew them in other lifetimes. For, you see, your dogs and cats know they live in many dimensions at once. In other words, they know they are carrying on several lifetimes all at the same time. When they are asleep in your dimension they are awake and aware in some other dimension. They might even be carrying on a lifetime on the other side of the world. All of it is to get the greatest bang for the buck, so to speak.

We human beings also live multidimensional lives, but we are far less aware we are doing so when we are focused in our physical bodies. The reason, I suspect, is that we use our rational thinking and logical brains to stay focused in one life, and we would become confused if we were to carry that rational, logical, linear thinking into several places at once. Therefore we shut off the other activities and focus on only one thing at a time. Animals, on the other hand, rely more on the feeling portion of their consciousness than on the logical rational portion. They therefore can be in several places and doing several different things at once without being confused at all.

I know one thing for certain: The longer I am away from the earth, the more I am convinced we human beings got the evolutionary scale all backwards. If you look at what human beings know and what they do compared to the other life forms on the planet, it would seem human beings must be at the bottom of the evolutionary scale, followed by the animals, and then the plants, and then the rocks. And if you wonder why a rock should be the highest form of life on earth, think about what a rock does. It does nothing. It has developed the art of just "being" to the ultimate.

PART III

ADAPTING TO A
NEW REALITY

Chapter Nine

Going Through Childhood Again

One of the major differences between life on earth and life here in the afterlife is that life on earth is much more predictable than it is in the nonphysical realms of the afterlife. We all come into the earth realm as babies and take about twenty years to grow through childhood and adolescence to adulthood, where we finally can go out and live with a sense that we have achieved a mastery of our environment.

In the nonphysical realms of the afterlife I was astounded to discover we come in at all different levels, and our progress through "childhood" to "adulthood," or mastery of the nonphysical environment, is unique to each of us.

Some of us who have just arrived here are like little children learning how to manipulate our world, just as earth children are learning how to manipulate physical reality. Others, like myself, seem to arrive already adapted to nonphysical life, having acclimated ourselves through the exploration of these realms in altered states of consciousness before we left the earth.

In every case the adaptation comes surprisingly easily with a little practice. In fact, it seems to me the learning curve to adapt to the nonphysical realms is much faster and easier than it is in learning to operate a human body in the physical dimension of earth. If we had linear time here, we could compare our system to yours as being a matter of weeks instead of the several years you find necessary to acclimate yourself to human reality.

In many ways I truly do feel like a child again, having that sense of eye bulging surprise at everything that comes into my senses. Each day brings brand new events I have never experienced before, and I feel as though I am going around all the time saying, "Wow!!! Isn't that neat!!" At the same time I sometimes feel frustrated: Because there is so much here that is so strange and different, it can feel overwhelming.

When we first arrive here in this realm, we have a body much like the one we have just left behind on earth. I should say it looks the same, but it does not feel the same. On earth, for example, I was suffering from cancer and my body was racked with pain. When I arrived here I no longer had the pain. Also, when I was in the transitory period between the earth realm and this realm, it felt as though I grew larger and lighter when my consciousness came here, and then I would feel as if I were shrinking, contracting and becoming extremely heavy when I would slip back into my physical existence. That distinction went away after I left the earth for good and stayed here. I then went through the incubation period and came out feeling quite "normal" in my new body.

On the other hand, I noticed my new body felt much lighter than it had ever felt to me on earth. There was not this feeling of being weighted down. I remember thinking to myself that I felt as the astronauts must have felt when they landed on the moon in 1969 and were bouncing around on the moon's surface at only one-sixth of their normal earth weight. If I were to guess, I would say these realms felt as if they had about one-tenth of the amount of gravity on earth. And that was just at first, for as I got used to it, I found the gravity kept reducing as I learned other ways to move about.

Whereas you live in a realm dominated by physical sensation, I live in a realm where the mind and the spirit reign supreme. Unlike your world, which is solid and relatively stable, mine is more fluid in nature. In fact, as I have evolved to new states of consciousness, my outer world has become much less solid and much more fluid than when I first arrived here from my deathbed. You might say my world is now more like a body of water or sometimes even a thin gaseous atmosphere. At least it seems I do not rely on gravity as much as I used to when I was just a newborn to this realm. Now I don't feel gravity at all.

When we first come to the afterlife, we are given the opportunity to create our own dwelling place. It gives us something familiar and comfortable to reside in until we expand our consciousness and are ready to move to other dimensions. It also gives us an opportunity to practice using our minds to create our reality and to see our reality burst forth the instant we think it into existence.

You create in the same manner with your human consciousness, but the process is much slower because your creations have to slow down from the frequency of mental thought into the density of solid matter so that you can perceive your creations with your physical senses.

Here the process is instantaneous. It is much like having a computer program with an infinite number of colors and an infinite number of drawing tools to play with. We then take our mental "mouse" and start designing whatever we desire, and we see instantly the results of our creativity and imagination. Because I loved the ocean in my lifetime as Susan Wells, I found great pleasure in creating an ocean for myself when I first came here. I then created a little cottage that sits next to a beach looking out on the water toward the west, where I can create beautiful sunsets anytime I desire.

At first our world of the afterlife looks much like the planet earth, for most if not all the beings I've met here have passed into these realms from lifetimes recently ended on earth. You could say our dimension is a nonphysical replica of the planet earth, but it is different in several respects. For one thing, it doesn't look as "solid" here as it does in your world. Perhaps that is because we know we can move our consciousness instantly from one place to another without having to pick up a heavy body and move it around.

Since there is nothing solid for us to hang onto nor gravity to hold us onto a floor or a chair, we are merely floating in place. We get this feeling of undulation as we float in place because our energy is vibrating at slightly different frequencies throughout our bodies. We get used to the sensation rather quickly because it is always that way for us, just as you get used to the sensation of gravity and the feeling of sitting or standing still. In truth, you too are in constant motion. You just don't feel it because you have trained yourself to ignore it.

If you have ever spent a long time on a ship, you will know what I mean. At first you feel as though you are bobbing up and down all the time, and walking is difficult unless you have something to hold onto in order to maintain your balance. In time, you get used to the constant undulating motion and no longer feel it. But when you return to land once more, the solid unyielding ground feels strange to you, and you have trouble walking until you get your "land legs" back again.

On earth the solid physical matter all around you gives you a stable environment in which to operate. But your inner world is always in motion. You are constantly creating pictures in your mind as someone speaks to you or tells you a story. You can be sitting in a room and let your thoughts roam all over the place. The next thing you know, your thoughts are far away from where they started out. Then if you realize you have allowed your mind to stray, you can instantly return your focus to the solid outer world where you were before you began your mental excursion. And you will note the room that surrounds you stayed the same while you were cavorting through the realms of your mind.

In the afterlife our outer world is not as stable. Since it is being created by our thoughts in the moment we are thinking it, our outer world shifts as soon as we shift our thoughts. Thus if we are scattering our thoughts around, we will end up in constant motion, moving to one place and then another in rapid succession. There is nothing to stop us from going off in any direction into any part of the universe just by thinking about it. There is no space or time here to make us think it will take a certain amount of time to travel a certain amount of space. In the afterlife we can go here, there, and everywhere, and it takes no traveling to get there.

It was this fluidity of the outer world that was hard to get used to when I first discovered these realms from my deathbed. Like every other human being, I was used to the solidity and stability of my outer world on earth. The feeling I had was similar to the feeling you get in some amusement park rides when they place you in an enclosed capsule and then show a movie that surrounds you and gives you the sensation you are moving rapidly through the scene. It makes for a marvelous ride, and the whole experience can be exciting—for a few minutes at least. But now just try to imagine if your whole world were like that. And imagine further if you were the one creating the rapid motion with your own thoughts.

To reiterate, the major difference between your reality and mine is that you can move yourself and your thoughts all around the place, but your outer world remains relatively stable. Even when you are driving yourself around in your automobile and you see the scenery flying by outside your windows, you can still focus your attention far enough in front of you to give you the feeling you are moving through your outer world while your outer world is staying in the same place.

In the afterlife I have the opposite feeling. It is as though I am the one who stays in the same place and my outer world goes moving all around me, either fast or slow, but always in motion. My own focus of consciousness controls how fast or slow the scene moves or even what scene it is.

The transport from one scene to the next feels like a flashing off of one scene and a flashing on of another. If we take our thoughts off the scenery in our outer world, it will evaporate before our eyes to be replaced with new scenery in keeping with our new thoughts. If we want to maintain the same scenery, we have to focus and concentrate real hard to keep it in place.

Many of us feel a sense of disorientation and frustration when we first arrive here because our scenery keeps changing. While it is no big deal to recreate it if we lose it, still, it can be distracting, especially if we are just trying to maintain a backdrop to our main activity. After a period of slipping and sliding around we realize our outer world is just a backdrop and not truly necessary to the task at hand. Hence we begin to realize the advantage of having an outer world that constantly readjusts to our thoughts. It certainly makes long arduous travel a thing of the past. Think of a place and—poof!—we're there.

Even so, this dimension takes some getting used to, and we must stay close to our teachers and guides until we can develop our own internal guidance system. This guidance is necessary, for if we were to stray too far away, we might become lost in a reality system in which we could not operate. We could then frighten ourselves to such an extent that we could be lost for some time and it would be difficult for our teachers or guides to find us and rescue us. You see, even in these realms where we supposedly have total freedom, we are still like little children who must have some restraints placed on them. Otherwise we might find ourselves in the equivalent situation of falling into the swimming pool and drowning or running out into the middle of the street and being run over by a car.

I become curious about something and the next thing I know I'm off exploring. And then I find myself going off in several directions at once. Flicker off here, flicker on there, flicker on somewhere else, flicker, flicker, flicker, going faster and faster until it all ends up a whirlwind of scenes flashing by. The only way I can stop it is to draw back from it into myself to shut down my mental activity. Then I can start over again, only in a much more focused manner. It's all a matter of being able to hold my focus at a particular vibratory frequency so that I don't slide around or even slide away into some other part of the universe. Sometimes it has become so chaotic that my teachers have had to rescue me. What they must do is to follow me, attract my attention, hook onto my energy, and then bring me back.

Our outer world also flickers when other people are involved. On earth you usually see other people moving into your presence when they arrive or moving away when they leave. In the afterlife others seem to suddenly materialize or disappear. On the other hand, it does not appear that they materialize or disappear directly from the scenes we are creating with our thoughts. It's more like a mutual decision to be in a scene together. Thus we all seem to appear simultaneously in the same scene.

For example, I can be sitting here with two friends, A and B. Then C, who has been somewhere else, thinks of us and decides to join us. It does not appear to us that A and B and I are sitting here and then all of a sudden C materializes. Instead it is as though the whole scene flickers and then we're in a new scene where A and B and C are now with me. It then feels to me as if this scene has been going on all along.

Then if C decides to go elsewhere, the whole scene flickers to a new scene, and then there are just A and B and I again, and it feels as though that scene has been going on all along. But then if we remember C was here, and if we want C to rejoin us, we only need to focus our thought on C. The scene flickers and C reappears. Once again, as soon as C reappears, it feels as though C has been with us all along.

I am not trying to suggest this reality is completely foreign to your own senses, for you are doing something similar to this in your dreams. You can find yourself moving through the scenery in your dreams in a manner similar to the way we move around in our realm. In addition, you can be doing something in a dream and, all of a sudden, you will think of someone and they will instantly appear. You will then be so focused in the current scene that you will forget there was ever another scene preceding this one.

Perhaps the dream state is one mechanism we provide for ourselves while we are living our lives as human beings to keep us in practice so that we will not be completely disoriented when we leave the earth and our physical bodies behind and come back here to live in the nonphysical realms of the afterlife.

Finally, we can even experience our reality from two or more perspectives at once. We can focus our attention here or there, or both, or everywhere at once.

You see, we don't have restraints on our time here as you do there. I can be on my merry way doing what I'm doing, and then others can come along and invite me to participate with them. I can partition my consciousness, so to speak, and focus a portion of my attention to their activities while at the same time still continuing with my other endeavors with the other parts of my consciousness.

That really should not be such a strange concept to most of you, for you have all trained yourselves quite nicely to be doing two or three things at once. For example, you can eat and watch television at the same time. You can also drive a car down the highway and talk to a passenger or telephone a friend at the same time.

The only difference is that, when you divide your focus, you have a tendency to pay less attention to each of the things you are doing. Here our consciousness can be focused fully in each place or activity in which we are engaged.

I think it has to do with our consciousness being free of the limitations imposed on you by your physical nature. As you know, scientists say you use only about ten percent of your mental capacity. This seems to be a limitation imposed by your DNA, which shuts down portions of your brain and allows you to perceive your reality in an extremely narrow range. Otherwise you would not be able to concentrate on anything at all, and your world as you perceive it would fly apart at the seams.

At this point I am much more aware of my multidimensional nature and can actually focus on dozens of things at once. I suppose you could say I learned how to do this through practice, first by learning to focus in two dimensions and then by adding more dimensions as I went along.

But I don't want to convey the impression that practice is all that is involved. Instead I believe it is a developmental trait we obtain simply by being in this dimension. The closest analogy to your situation I can think of is the human skill of walking. Yes, a baby has to learn how to walk, and she seems to require a lot of practice until she gets good at it. But it is in the nature of being human to walk, and the baby would eventually walk anyway even if no one were to teach her.

When we have finally gotten used to this floating, flickering and multidimensional experiencing of our outer world, our childhood comes to an end. We are then ready to explore our own and other realms in the afterlife with a sense of mastery.

Chapter Ten

Losing Track of Time

*H*ere in the afterlife we quickly lose track of your time altogether. I have no idea by now how long I have been here. In a way, it seems as though it has been forever and my forty-four years as Susan Wells was just a flash—or perhaps a dream. At other times I feel as though I just arrived here yesterday. For a while after I had first arrived here I tried to keep track of your time, but that became impossible in short order.

For one thing, none of us goes around wearing watches on our wrists, nor do we have clocks on the wall. The idea of clocks and other devices to measure intervals or units of distance between events is a human concept we invented in order to move about in the physical plane.

We lose track of the "time," not only because we have no clocks, but also because we have a different cycle between events. We don't have a sense of day and night or a division of our time between sleeping and waking, as you do. Therefore we don't have a sense of events moving through time.

I'm not saying time just vanishes the moment you throw away your physical body and come here. There are some who feel more comfortable when they first arrive here if they can create conditions that are familiar to themselves from their previous life on earth. Thus you will find them leading rigidly scheduled routines, doing one thing for a certain interval, and then doing another thing for an relatively equal interval. As they become comfortable with the variety of modes here, they let loose and free themselves gradually from the rigidity. There are others who come here and just hang out, acting as though they never had any sense of time on earth either.

Your sense of time is also cultural. Some countries in your world are much more tied to the clock than others. It is the same here. But here we have much greater freedom to choose for ourselves and to not be locked into a cultural scheme.

If you think about it, the cyclical nature of events on earth causes you to perceive your time in a linear fashion. You wake up from your dream state every morning, and you find yourself in your bed getting ready to face yet another "day" in your life. The sun has perhaps come up and is slowly moving across the sky. Things are happening all around you on which you focus your attention; you get a sense of time elapsing between each of these events. As you go on about your day, you are always refocusing your attention from one thing to the next. Thus time moves for you.

You realize you consistently spend about a third of your twenty-four-hour day asleep and two-thirds awake. Hence you have a steady pattern by which you can measure time. You also have different events in your world which help you to measure time, such as your sun's movement across your sky, your moon's revolution around your planet, and your planet's revolution around your sun. These define your days, months, and years for you. Over the history of your various civilizations you have created more and more ways to measure these various cycles, and with the invention of your various time measuring devices, you have become more and more cognizant of time.

The concept of time has changed in the different eras of your earth history as well. It was only in the past hundred years that human beings became so conscious of "the time" that they started wearing watches to know "what time it is" and started organizing their lives according to schedules. I suppose it was inevitable that humankind would come along and organize it and make a lot of rules about it.

Many of you order your lives not only by your waking and sleeping cycles, but also by your working, commuting, and television program schedules. Many of you have even trained yourselves to raid your refrigerators and go to the bathroom during your work breaks and your TV commercials. You find yourselves governed by your time pieces, for your various units of time measurement are all around you. In your society this has made time an object in and of itself.

But what do you suppose would happen if you were to leave your watch on the bedside stand and take down all the clocks, calendars, and other devices that tell you the "time"? What if you were to be stranded on an island where there was no "time"? You would soon lose track of what day it is. You would not know exactly what "time" it is either. Yet you would still have a feeling of movement between the events in your life. Here we see time as a much more fluid property. Thus we are not as conscious of time as you are.

You have been taught that time is the distance between two events. Your technological world has then made sure that events are equally spaced apart so that time could be flattened into a straight linear function. But if you were to go off to that hypothetical island without all the clocks, calendars, and other paraphernalia of your time-ordered world, you would soon find time is much more variable. You would find time sometimes moves quickly and sometimes moves slowly. At times it does not move at all and occasionally it seems to disappear and then comes back into your awareness several minutes or hours later.

For me time dragged excruciatingly slowly when I was lying in my sick bed, all riddled with the pain of cancer. On the other hand, when I was on morphine to suppress the pain, I felt great pockets of time disappear. I would be lying there thinking it was early morning and find to my great surprise that it was late afternoon.

The movement of the earth around the sun gives you a sense of time. You feel motion, both in your spatial dimension and in your temporal dimension. Here we feel all this and more. Time can move and stop simultaneously for us.

We move from one activity to another and change pace as we go along to maintain an equilibrium. But this change of pace is not quite as formal and rigid as is your habit of waking and sleeping. We have no regular intervals of light and dark outside—it's always day here. Or we can create it to be always night too, I suppose.

For many of you, when you go to sleep at night, you may not experience the same sense of time moving as you do throughout the day because your consciousness goes someplace else. You don't remember where you have been or what you were doing while your body was sleeping away in your bed. Thus, for many of you, the last thing you focus on is lying in your bed in the dark and falling asleep. Then the next event is your waking up again the next morning. The only way you can tell time has elapsed is to look at your clock. You then tell yourself, "Oh, yeah. I went to bed at 11:00 last night, and now here it is 7:00 this morning, so eight hours must have passed." Then you get a feeling about that eight hours based on your memory of other eight-hour periods you have spent when you were fully awake and consciously focusing on one event after another. Thus you mentally tell yourself how long that eight hours of sleep lasted, and you then begin to feel you were in your bed for a long time.

But, in truth, unless you were lying there half awake all night focusing a part of your consciousness on events in your outer world as you were sleeping, or perhaps got up to go to the bathroom during the night, you would feel as though no time had elapsed during the night.

In the afterlife we can play with the idea of linear time elapsing if we choose. We can act out a scenario and create events to occur which will give us the feeling of sequence from one event to another. To make this elapsing of time feel even more "linear," we can create our outer world more solidly. But the difference between our doing this and your experiencing your linear time is that we know we are only creating the effect as we go along. In other words, we are consciously aware we are focusing on only one event at a time and then moving from event to event in sequence, whereas you do so unconsciously.

Time becomes fluid and malleable here. You lost that perception of time when you started focusing on time as a linear external object. Here we see it more as an internal feeling we can manipulate and rearrange any way we please. We can make time go forward or backward, move up or down, move inside out or outside in. We can associate time with color or sound or any number of other "senses." We can slow it down or speed it up, or do both at the same time. You see, our concept of time is to your concept of time as our concept of space is to your concept of space. You tend to view both as "solid" matter. We see time and space as different frequency waves we can flow through.

Although we still have a concept of one event following another if we choose to view two or more events in such a linear fashion, we can also reconstruct the notion of time as all-encompassing instead of linear. That is, we can tune in on all events happening simultaneously in the here and now. We can even be in several places at once and be conscious of them all. Moreover, we can be in several places at the same time, and time can be marching along at a different speed in each of those places.

This is all difficult to describe to you in terms you can understand because we don't have the same sense of time and space that you do. Everything I do in the present moment seems as though I've been doing it forever, until I stop to explore that idea and then I realize I have also been elsewhere doing other things at the same time.

If you wanted to, you could experiment with focusing your attention on several things at once, of taking yourself out of your sense of linear time and viewing your world in a more spatial than linear fashion. In this way of focusing, you would see everything as occurring right here and right now in the eternally present moment, and you would ignore the movement of your conscious focus from one event to another. In your realm this seems strange indeed. In fact, many of you cannot bring yourselves into this state of spatial time for more than a few seconds before your consciousness wants to drift away again and find another event upon which to focus.

Many of you have become slaves to your time pieces. Workaholism runs rampant through your society as you try to accomplish more and more in less and less time. You'll be happy to know, there is no such thing as time pressure in the afterlife. We realize we have all eternity if we desire to accomplish anything we want. I'm hoping you will take these words to heart, that your lives may become less hectic, and that you may find some rest and relaxation for yourselves. For you have all eternity as well. The trick is to stay focused in the here and now as much as you can, because here and now is truly all there is.

Chapter Eleven

Our New Bodies

*W*hen we first arrive here in the afterlife, we have a new body, but we don't question where it came from or how we obtained it. For the most part, the body we start out with here is similar to the one we left behind on earth. But it rapidly grows more functional and whole. In my case, the body I left behind had been all riddled with cancer and many of my internal organs had been eaten away. I had no strength left in those last few days, and I had lost all control of my bodily functions.

While my body was deteriorating in that lifetime, I was already forming a new body for myself in this realm. While I was wasting away there, I was healing and growing stronger here.

At first, my new body here was still solid, but not as solid as my earthly body had been. I felt lighter in weight because there was less gravity here. Quickly afterward, and especially after I pulled the plug on my earth life as Susan Wells, I evolved into a new body that was even lighter and more pliable. If I had to compare it to the elements you have on earth, I would say I went from being a solid body to a liquid. If you had been standing next to me with your solid physical body, you could have poked your hand right through me.

After I came out of my incubation period, my body underwent yet another transformation. This time I will carry the analogy a bit further and say that my body went from a liquid state to a heavy gaseous state. There was still some substance to my body that felt more "solid" than my surroundings, but not very much.

This does not mean that my body did not have a feeling of integrity. It still felt as though there were boundaries between my body and my surroundings. But even those boundaries have become hazy as my body continues to evolve.

When I say that my boundaries are hazy, I'm referring to the outermost region of my body, which includes what you would call the aura. And here is where there is a major difference between my body here in the afterlife and the body I left behind on earth. Having an aura means that I "glow" with color and light as I radiate the essence of myself. I'm becoming more translucent but more colorful, you might say. My friends and associates can all see my aura and know exactly what I am thinking and feeling, for as I think and feel, I radiate different colors. Even though you radiate colorful auras around your human bodies too, few of you have the sensitivity to perceive auras around each other.

While I realize there are some psychics and very sensitive human beings who can feel the edge of another's aura, for the most part, you tend to believe the boundaries of your body are around the surface of your skin. This is true even though there is a culturally defined "space" around yourself that is taboo to intrude on when you are standing close to another. When someone invades your space by getting too close to you, you feel uncomfortable because they have invaded your aura.

As our bodies lose their solidity and become "light as air," there is truly no need to connect to a ground anymore. Nor do we need to walk about in order to get from one place to another. Instead, our mobility is all mental. Therefore I usually am not even aware of having any legs or feet anymore. I am now beginning to present myself in a new body that arises out of nothingness and just floats about.

And now I realize I have reached the stage of evolution of those beings who I noticed had no feet when I first made my sojourns here from my deathbed. I remember then how strange it seemed for them to arise out of nothingness. I remember thinking to myself, this must be where the human depiction of ghosts and apparitions came from. Isn't this a hoot! I've now become your friendly Casper the Ghost!

That is, when I have a body at all. There are times when having a body becomes an inconvenience. True, it can be a wonderful vehicle to plop myself into so that I can absorb and feel the energies around me. But I think that must be just a carryover from human consciousness, which relies very much on its body to be the receptor and the measuring device for the energies it perceives. Here it isn't necessary. My mental or even my spiritual consciousness can perceive energies just as well as, and perhaps even better than, a body can.

We don't need to sleep here in the afterlife as you do on earth. The primary reason is that we do not have to contend with lugging around a heavy body all day long in a dense world. Just moving your body around all day is a strenuous job, and for that reason you have to put your body to bed every night so that it can regenerate itself. Here our bodies don't have to contend with gravity, especially after we have been here for a while and have become acclimated to the nonphysical environment. When we feel comfortable moving around in our nonphysical bodies, we can maneuver them effortlessly. There is no resistance whatsoever in any part of our environment.

At this point my memory of having been in a physical body with its constraints and its feeling of heaviness—even its pain and other physical sensations—is slipping away ever so gently. It's similar to your experience when you are pregnant. For the nine months that you are carrying the baby around inside you, you feel at times as though this is the norm and you will be pregnant for the rest of your life. You even begin to forget what it was like not to be pregnant. Then you have your baby, and a few months or a few years later, you can hardly remember what it felt like to have been pregnant.

We all have that experience when we are passing back and forth from the physical realms of earth to the nonphysical realms of the afterlife. Wherever we are focused is what seems "real," and the other experience fades away into a memory. There are some realms in which you become so focused—and I am speaking of earth life now—that you believe it is the only realm you have *ever* experienced and is the only realm there is. Believing that, you cannot even imagine what it would be like to be going around without a physical body. You believe your self-awareness must dissipate without skin to form a boundary and to separate yourself from your surroundings. You get these images in your mind that you would have no substance whatsoever or that you would somehow become invisible.

We can have any kind of "body" we want here. There are some who prefer to create themselves quite solidly, and they go around in an outer world that is relatively solid. They follow many of the same rules that you do on earth. That is, they don't go through walls, they can't see through solid objects, they move from one place to another by walking their body there, or they even create vehicles in which to transport themselves.

They create bodies for themselves that look human in all respects, including the gender they were in their prior life. They can, of course, make any modifications to their body—and many of them do—to make themselves younger and more active, for instance. Most revert to an age when they were in their prime, whatever that may mean to them individually. Thus some revert to their early twenties, while others prefer the late twenties or early thirties. Still others remain at somewhat older ages; say, in their sixties, because they feel a sense of greater wisdom and serenity than they may have remembered feeling at younger ages.

Interestingly, not many choose to be children or teenagers here, perhaps because they remember those periods in their previous earth life to have been more difficult or less pleasant than adulthood. Even those who come here as children or teenagers seem to move quickly into adulthood in the afterlife.

There are other realms here where the beings have bodies that look like human bodies, but their bodies appear much less solid. They seem more transparent and they can flash in or out of the scenery. These beings can either create earth-type clothing for themselves through their thoughts or they will simply drape themselves in color.

There are still other dimensions here where the beings will create bodies, but they will have moved beyond the concept of gender, as you know it. In other words, they will be more unisex, and you cannot tell from looking at them if they are male or female—nor does that seem odd.

Finally, there are realms here where the beings become amorphous and—well, ghostly. That is, if I were to look at them, I would get only the faintest impression that someone is here. There might be a wisp of energy or a slight color change. Yet I know someone is here, for their personality is quite obvious. In other words, I can feel their "presence."

I can communicate with these beings just fine, for, at that level, all communication is by mental telepathy. There is no need to "see" them or to "hear" them speak. When I encounter them, I know I need only move into their energy and blend with them. I can then know everything in their mind and they can know everything in mine.

What I'm trying to convey here—and I hope not too clumsily—is that I have been moving away from the idea of sight, sound, touch, taste, and smell as the only ways to perceive. As a matter of fact, I'm beginning to see that those senses you have as human beings are quite crude compared to the senses we have here. This is a bit difficult to explain, but I will do my best, because I want you to understand that there are other senses than the ones you have become familiar with as human beings. But I have a problem describing these senses to you so that you can understand them. It's as though a sighted person were trying to describe color to a blind person or a hearing person were trying to tell a deaf person what it sounds like when the waves come crashing in upon the shore and the sea gulls are singing to each other. What I can tell you is that our senses give us far more information about our outer world than do your senses about your outer world.

We can also create new bodies for ourselves at any time, and that is another major difference between our world and yours. You go into your world as a human being and you live your entire lifetime as a human being. True, your body changes as you grow from infancy to adulthood and then advance to old age, but you still have a feeling of continuity with your body as you move from day to day or even possibly from year to year.

In the afterlife we are not limited to just one body for a so-called lifetime. We can change our body into something else with just a passing thought. I can be solid or not. I can project a male or female gender, or neither. I can be a human being or any other life form, either "real" or imagined. I can be a geometric shape, or a color, or even nothing at all. That is to say, I can become "invisible" and you wouldn't know I was here unless I would choose to project an energy you could perceive.

I am also not just limited to a body you can "see." I can be a sound or a variety of sounds. I can be a smell or a taste. I can be something that can be perceived by other senses you don't even know about because they are not within the range of senses with which you are familiar. If I get tired of one body, I can don another.

It is this great variety in the nonphysical realms of the afterlife that distinguishes them from the physical realms of earth. The combinations and permutations are limitless. Whatever my mind can imagine, I can be. Be a tree? Sure. Easy! Be a star? Why not? A geometric shape that has ninety-seven sides but no inside or outside? I'll try anything at least once! It gives new meaning to the expression, "You can be anything you want to be," wouldn't you say? For you must also remember I am not limited to your concepts of time and space anymore. It's all right here. It's all right now. It's All-That-Is. I can be any part of it or all of it. There are no limits.

I also want to point out that my perception of my own body is only my perception based on what I believe. I then project outward what I believe to be my body from within myself so that others can perceive me. But what they perceive and what I project may be entirely different. For example, I am now projecting myself as a wispy, almost-as-light-as-air phantom that can appear and disappear, grow more or less bright, and radiate different hues. Another being might come along and see me as a solid body, much as they remember a human being should look like. Hence their image of me will derive from their belief, not mine.

This is not much different from your experience on earth. But I will concede that the differences between what you project as your body image and the body image someone else perceives of you are more similar to each other. For example, let us say you are a 125-pound woman, thirty-five years old, who has an image of herself as old and fat. Another person might come along, say, a fifty-year-old woman weighing 150 pounds, who may perceive you as young and thin.

It is not just weight or age that you perceive, but also height, health, beauty, even your hair style, or the way you wear your clothes. You have all seen a fat lady walking down the street wearing a pair of tight stretch pants that you think looks hideous on her when you see her from behind. You wonder how she can possibly stand to be dressed like that in public. Perhaps it is because this fat lady perceives her own body quite differently, even thinking she looks slim and svelte in her tight pants. And then there is the opposite effect of the fat person wearing what she thinks is a loose flowing dress that others think looks like a circus tent. On the other hand, we all have known anorexics who have starved themselves down to an emaciated skeleton because they thought of themselves as horribly fat.

The point I'm trying to make is that my body as I perceive it is not necessarily what others see when they see me. Nor does it matter. At least the beings here are not as judgmental as they are on earth, although I will also tell you that your body image obsessions are very much a twentieth-century American phenomenon, certainly a quirk in the overall history of the earth. Much of it is a mechanism for one group of people to gain power over another group.

Our bodies seem to be driven more by thought, although I recognize that the human body is driven by thought as well. That is, first you form an intention to do something or to move about somewhere, and your body follows suit. Many of you don't even think about it because you have your thoughts and your attention focused elsewhere. It's as though your body goes on automatic pilot for you. But your body will not move about by itself without your telling it what to do. You are the one in charge of its overt activities in your outer world.

On the other hand, your body carries out thousands of functions internally that you are not even aware of. By this I mean that your body maintains itself and keeps itself "alive" by breathing, circulating blood, manufacturing chemicals, warding off diseases, and reproducing cells continually.

Here in the afterlife it seems as though our bodies do even more "automatic pilot" stuff. We don't have to be concerned about staying healthy, for instance. We don't have to feed our bodies or rest them. All those functions are necessary only in the physical dimension of earth where certain biological laws must be followed. You have to constantly tend to your bodies in order to keep them "alive." Here we have laws that keep our bodies "alive," but these laws are not biological. The bodies that we have here are virtually "maintenance free."

Actually, it does not feel as though our lifestyle is that different from yours. But when I think about it some more I realize that it is extremely different. I've become quite comfortable here, so it seems as if I have always been nonphysical. As time goes on, I'm beginning to forget what it was like to have a physical human body, and that truly does amaze me.

All in all, when you ask whether we have bodies here, my answer would have to be: "It depends."

Chapter Twelve

Friends, Neighbors, and Society

There are many levels of consciousness in the afterlife. People who come here will transfer into different levels based on their understanding and beliefs when they leave the earth. Thus many of us first come into a realm similar to the earth in many respects. At this entry level there is solid matter much like that on earth, except it does not look or feel as dense.

After our arrival we will stay in the more solid realms for differing periods, depending on our beliefs and desire to move upward in our evolution. But we cannot stay in the solid realms forever. In every level of existence there are teachers and guides who are constantly encouraging us to explore and to move our consciousness to greater awareness. There is also an innate drive in each of us to grow and to expand our consciousness.

To say that someone would desire to stay at a particular level of existence for a long time would be like saying a five-year-old wants to stay five years old for a long time. No, after a period of time the five-year-old is anxious to become six years old, and then seven, and then someday a grownup. We all want to continue growing in understanding and wisdom.

At the risk of contradicting myself, however, I will say I have observed some here who seem to be stuck in a particular place. These beings usually have been so shut away from their spiritual source that they truly believe where they are is where they will be forever, and there is nothing else.

Some of these beings led the proverbial lives of quiet desperation on earth and carried that desperation with them when they crossed over here after death. Many do not know they have "died" and think they are still alive on earth. Many, if not most, of them believe they are insane.

It is sad to see these beings, for many seem to lead lives of squalor and hopeless despair. They don't seem to understand where they are or what they are doing. When we try to talk to them, they seem to be in tremendous fear and distrust. They keep to themselves and hide from others. Most of the time they seem to have a form of "blinders" on, and they tune out all but the awareness of themselves alone.

But being alone is an illusion they create for themselves, for none of us is ever truly alone. There are all sorts of teachers and guides who are constantly around each of us, watching out for us. You have teachers, guides, and guardian angels surrounding you at all times too.

In contrast to those who come into the lower, more solid realms of the afterlife, there are others who transfer into the higher realms where life is quite different from the life they left behind on earth. These beings will most likely have been on a life-long quest for spiritual growth and will have engaged in spiritual practices, such as meditation, prayer, astral travel, lucid dreaming, channeling, and developing close ties with their teachers and guides in the spirit world.

When they leave the earth behind, they are consciously aware they are creating their own transition from one state of consciousness to another. They choose the circumstances of their death and go through it with a great sense of fun and adventure.

They have no fear of death whatsoever. Instead they see it as the great adventure that it truly is. They then pass into the afterlife knowing quite well where they are going, and they call on the powers of the universe to assist them in their journey. They never have a sense of being alone, but instead see themselves as a part of an entire group consciousness, similar to the way an ant sees itself as a part of its colony and knows what every other ant in its colony is experiencing.

These beings often make a grand exit from the earth and an even grander entrance into the afterlife in a homecoming ceremony that commands the attention of the entire universe. When they arrive here, they have no trouble acclimating to the new rules, for they have been rehearsing in their meditations and in their dreams long before they arrived. They slide into the nonphysical arena, not as babies or children, but as full grown adults, so to speak. If there is any incubation period or acclimation period, it is over with in a flash. Boom! Flicker off in the physical awareness, flicker on in the nonphysical awareness ready to don their light bodies and go exploring All-That-Is.

Surprisingly, I do not see a large "population" of beings here and may not ever run into them. The reason is that the number of "places" here is virtually infinite. You know how large your planet is with its nearly six billion people roaming around on it. Yet some of you never run into more than a few hundred or at most a few thousand of those billions of people in your whole lifetime there. The earth is a mere speck in the solar system, let alone the universal scheme of things. So you can imagine by comparison how "big" the afterlife is. Just as each of you is creating your own little world on earth, each of us is creating our own little heaven in heaven.

Those who are of like consciousness will come to where my friends and I reside because they will be attracted to our energy and will be aligned with our beliefs. In other words, they will feel more comfortable here in the vibratory frequency that we are radiating.

There are some here who look like solid physical human beings, but then there are also nonphysical energies I can't see or touch. Yet I know they are here, for I can feel them with my inner senses.

There are also other life forms here I can see and touch, but they are not like any life forms I ever saw on earth. Some of them come here to investigate what earth living is all about, and they can take "classes" here to orient them and prepare them for incarnating into human bodies on earth. Others are just passing through, as though they are tourists exploring realms different from their own.

They will go back "home" again to their part of the universe and take with them nothing more than the memory of having visited here.

You see, the wonder of this place is its infinite variety. You can move through many different layers, passing from one realm to another, tasting the assorted colors and flavors of each realm. In the end it is all very simple. It is all God-All-That-Is experiencing itself in all its infinite diversity, each aspect exploring all the other aspects, but all realizing eventually it is all one consciousness.

Just as you have unseen beings hanging about you and observing what you are doing—even guiding you along your spiritual path—we also have unseen beings hanging around us. At every level of consciousness there is a feeling we are not alone and there is an awareness of unseen presences. Included in the menagerie of unseen entities are beings from other dimensions whose vibratory frequency is beyond our ability to perceive at this stage of our development.

In addition, we have our teachers and guides who are pulling on our energy to bring us to new heights of awareness. Of course, we also have our teachers and guides here in this realm that we can see, but they are more or less at the same level of consciousness and are operating from the same ground rules as we are. Oftentimes our teachers and guides in the dimensions above us are teaching both ourselves and our teachers at this level. In all cases these unseen teachers are attracting our attention, causing us to reach for their consciousness and to move our consciousness toward them.

I suppose if we did not have unseen teachers at the levels above us, we would not be motivated to grow and evolve. That is to say, if our teachers were always in the same dimension as ourselves, we would all stay in the same place and never move on to explore other dimensions.

In addition to our teachers and guides, we also have our soul and our higher self that are invisible to us, just as yours are to you. I'm sure this will be the case all the way up the line to God-All-That-Is. When we have seen everything there is to see, known everything there is to know, done everything there is to do, and we're at the last level just below the top level where God resides, we will still not be able to see God. God will always be that elusive, ineffable concept of All-That-Is.

You may be wondering if we have a "social life" here as we did on earth, since human beings are social creatures. You are not meant to be alone in your lifetime for long. True, many of you will create solitude for yourselves from time to time, especially if you are feeling the need to go within your inner self to reconnect with your spiritual source. You often need to be alone to do your best creative work and thinking.

But for the most part you surround yourselves with people. When you are a child, you have family members around you constantly to give you the things you need to sustain your life in a physical body. You are then trained from an early age to associate with others in your peer group, be they your siblings, those you play with, or those you go to school with.

By the time you reach adulthood and are free to take over the reins of your life, you are well indoctrinated in the belief that you will always have other people around you. Thus you create working situations in which you interact with others, and you go rushing into relationships in order to form new families. Throughout your life you maintain friends and acquaintances to spell off loneliness. Is it any wonder then that you would be curious about the social structure of the afterlife?

When we first arrive here the social structure is much the same as on earth, for I have already explained we have a period of time here when we are like little children acclimating ourselves to the new rules for manipulating our environment.

People often wonder whom they can expect to meet when they cross over to this side of the veil from earth life. As a matter of fact, a lot of it depends on whom they want to meet. There are some who go around looking up all the people they were related to or ever knew to see where they are and what happened to them. These visits can be fun at first, and they certainly do give a sense of security. We don't feel quite as disoriented if we can contact people we have known before.

Just because you may have been a close friend with Sally, with whom you shared lunch every day your last year of high school, however, it does not follow that Sally and you will be lunch buddies here. For you must remember, both you and Sally were playing a role with each other on earth for whatever reason you happened to come into each other's lives. In the meantime you and Sally might have gone off on separate paths and have changed so drastically by the time you catch up to each other again that you each would feel you hardly knew the other. Or, more likely, each of you might have different interests that will take you to different dimensions on this side of the veil, and there will be nothing you have in common to attract you together again.

If you look at this issue more closely, you might realize you and your friend, Sally, actually drifted off into different dimensions on earth after you graduated from high school and separated from each other. Your paths then may have gone off in different directions, never to cross again. For all that it meant to you, she could have been dead all along.

You will be far more likely to run into people with whom you had long involved relationships, such as close lifelong friends or family members. But just because someone was closely related to you on earth, it does not necessarily mean that person will hang around with you forever here in the afterlife.

There is often an expectation that your parents will be waiting here to greet you and to welcome you home, but that only presupposes they died before you. Even if they did die before you, just because they were your parents on earth, they will not likely carry on the same relationship or role with you here. For all practical purposes, you might consider the afterlife as a completely new "lifetime" in which there are new roles and new relationships to be explored.

At the same time, and by the same reasoning, you might not necessarily take up with any former spouses when you arrive here nor have any desire to hang around and wait for them if you left them back on earth. Some of you who have been married many times may be relieved to know you don't have to run into any of your ex-spouses if you don't want to.

It seems to me those we choose to hang around with here are ones that we hung around with in between other earth lives. I have the impression that we tend to wander around in groups, and that we then move back to the earth together—to be together or not, depending on what we choose before we go—and then we all drift back "home" to be together again when our earth lifetimes are over.

The factor which brings us together and keeps us together here is a bond of attraction that runs very deep. Some of the beings I now hang around with are ones I have known for thousands or millions of years (as you would measure time), and perhaps even forever. But that is not true of everyone in my society, for some are constantly drifting in and out of here as they move along their path of evolution.

When I think about it some more, however, I feel as though I have joined this group consciousness to which I belong relatively recently. That is, I'm one of the newcomers, not because I just arrived here from my earth life, but because I have been associated with other groups to which I was more closely aligned before, and now I'm feeling the tug to be with this current group for my further advancement.

We have many different types of relationships here, just as we did when we were living our lifetimes on earth. But some of the roles we play here have less importance and other roles have more importance than on earth.

As you can well imagine, marriage is one of the most important relationships on earth, for it provides a framework in which to reproduce the species. We were all programmed from our earliest childhood to grow up, find someone of the opposite sex, get married, and raise children spawned out of that marriage.

Here in the nonphysical realms of the afterlife, because we have no need to biologically reproduce ourselves, there is less need to form marital or parent-child relationships. Moreover, as we evolve to the higher realms and take on bodies that are less and less solid, we lose our association with a particular gender.

Because most of the beings here choose to identify themselves with what you would call your adult years, there is no necessity to form family units to raise children. When children come here from earth, they quickly "grow" their consciousness and their self identity into adulthood. Hence, unlike on earth, where the majority of the human population is still in childhood, almost the entire population here is in adulthood.

We do not have much in the way of sexual relationships here, for sexual activity as you know it is a phenomenon of physical bodies. Here the closest thing we have to sexual activity is the blending of two (or more, for that matter) beings in which they merge together as one being. Thus, not only do we have two bodies coming together, but also two minds and two souls. We soon come to believe that sexual activity as you know it pales by comparison.

I have heard there are places here where a lot of sexual activity as you know it still goes on. But those places are in the "lower" realms where the beings are still very much tied to the earth and believe they still have their physical bodies. Many of them were sex addicts on earth who did not work though their addictions before they died. They therefore have created a reality for themselves where they can continue to act out their addictive behavior. It is my understanding they will stay in those lower realms until they become tired of it and desire to put it all behind them and move on. Others are trying to find a way to return to physical lifetimes as soon as possible, so that they can have "real" bodies for sexual activity once again.

Does that mean beings here do not form close love relationships with other beings? Not necessarily. In fact, we find more of what you would call "cohabitation" by unrelated persons in this plane. But these relationships tend to be short-lived experiences. When these beings have learned the lessons they set out to learn together, their relationships break up and reassemble into other relationships.

Just as we did on earth, we often will come together in groups to perform a particular project together. For example, a number of us might be interested in learning about a particular subject. We will then form a group, attract a teacher to work with us, go off and create a little community for ourselves for the duration of the experience, and then scatter apart as soon as our goal has been accomplished.

At other times a group of beings might want to practice certain social roles in preparation for reincarnating into human lifetimes on earth. They might decide, for example, that they want to reincarnate as a rural community in the Scottish Highlands in the sixteenth century. They will create a replica of that locale in the nonphysical realms of the afterlife and put on what you might call a dress rehearsal. In doing so, they might rewrite or fine-tune the blueprint for their joint lives. They might implant into their cellular consciousness such little tidbits as, "Do this, but don't do that." "Watch out for this dude." "Make sure you always keep one eye peeled behind you if you want to live beyond the ripe old age of thirty." After they have worked out all the details, they will then leave *en masse* and incarnate into the physical lifetimes they have just been rehearsing.

One thing I have noticed about the afterlife is that I really don't care what people think anymore. That is a human—and human alone—perception and worry. Here we know all thoughts are out in the open for everyone to pick up on. Therefore everyone knows all our innermost secrets. And nobody cares a hoot. It makes for much more honest relationships on this side of the veil. There can be no lying here, for everyone would know when we were lying. So why bother?

There is also no trying to impress our neighbor or trying to inflate ourselves in their eyes. They already know who we are and what we are in all the lurid details, and they don't care. Even more astounding, they love us anyway.

I know many of you are working toward the same level of honesty, sincerity, and unconditional, nonjudgmental love in your lives on earth. But you still tend to see yourselves in that way and then have to go out into your society and be exposed to others who remain in their dysfunctional modes of behavior and judgmental thinking.

You are on earth to learn about social relationships from the perspective of your individuality. You see yourselves as separate and distinct individuals when you are ensconced in a physical body because you have defined boundaries that separate your bodies from others. But there are times, even when you are in your physical bodies, when you get a glimpse of blending and merging with others. One example is when two of you are making love to each other. You can become so wrapped up in the activity that you feel as if your two selves are merging and becoming one.

On this side of the veil, we take that idea and explore it much further. Since we can make our bodies here as solid or as non-solid as we like, we can experience ourselves as separate beings or as fully blended beings. To remain more separate we become more solid and use our solid bodies to define our boundaries, much as you do on earth.

When we want to experiment with merging two or more beings together, we become more non-solid so that our bodies can actually blend together to form a new being. We then can experience all our own self and the other's self combined. The new being formed from this union can then walk around or do anything else the two of us could do individually.

For example, if I have a brilliant analytical mind but cannot read music, and the other person has a wonderful talent as a pianist, we can blend together and combine our attributes. We will then become a being who is both brilliant and a wonderful musician. Perhaps the combination will also allow us to do something neither one of us could do alone. Perhaps now we can compose brilliant musical masterpieces as well as play them.

This phenomenon is called "synergy" in your world, and it is a wonderful phenomenon we explore all the time in the afterlife. We mix, blend, and merge with various and sundry other beings to see what kinds of combinations we can make and what sorts of synergy come out of the combination.

There seems to be no limit to this combining of beings to form new beings. Perhaps all beings that ever have been, are, or ever will be could be combined into a total being. I believe that is what we would call God, a being with all the talents, abilities, knowledge, love, and all the other characteristics of each of its individual elements, which creates a synergy infinite in scope and is able to see itself as one single consciousness.

This combining and recombining seems to be what God is all about. It comes together to view itself as one, and at the same time it breaks itself apart into each of its infinite facets, each of which has a consciousness of its own. Then it goes about combining and recombining those infinite aspects to experience what each of its various combinations feels like. It plays itself out in every combination and permutation of itself, learning new things about itself with each experience of itself as a different combination of elements. In the end, when it comes back together as one single consciousness, it sees itself differently because now it has learned something new about itself. In that respect, God is always becoming something else. The process never ends, as far as I can see.

Getting back to my own realm and to the more mundane aspects of my own existence, my friends and I play at this combining and blending only in a limited fashion compared to the combining and blending going on at the level of God. Each time we do this, we are expanding our consciousness.

Let's go back to our example of the brilliant analyst combining with the musician. In our combined state, I said that we experience ourselves as more than the aggregate of the two of us apart. After we experience that synergy and pull apart once again, we each go away with a memory of ourselves combined. In other words, we take away all the knowledge that we both had. Each of us is now a brilliant, analytical musician.

We each might then go and combine with yet another being. Let's say the next time I want to blend with an affectionate, nurturing, motherly type. When we combine, we will then both feel ourselves as brilliant, analytical, musical, affectionate, nurturing, and motherly. And when we part from each other, we will both carry away all those aspects individually, each of us ready to then go and find someone else to blend with.

As you can see, our expansion of consciousness can take place quite rapidly under these circumstances. Yet as rapidly as this takes place, it still is a mere drop of water in the ocean between ourselves and the levels closer to the concept of God as a single all-encompassing consciousness in all its glory.

So you ask if we have a social life here. Yes, we do. It is very powerful, as you can imagine. The thrill and the ecstasy arising out of the combining and blending of consciousness with others is so intense that I cannot put the experience into words that you as a human being could comprehend. If I were to ask you to imagine the absolutely most thrilling and ecstatic thing you could ever do as a human being, you would probably imagine some kind of sexual experience, or perhaps some illicit drug experience. But the experience I am talking about is many times more intense than either of those.

On the other hand, I don't want you to come away with the impression that all we do all day is run around like ants in a colony, skittering hither and yon, bumping into each other, blending with them, saying, "Aaaahhh!" and then unhooking once more only to run around helter skelter to find the next being with whom we will blend. This sort of crazed running around is a bit too orgiastic to describe what really goes on.

We do not take this lightly. We choose carefully with whom we want to blend. Otherwise we could find ourselves taking on characteristics we don't necessarily want to have for ourselves. Just as on your planet in your human societies, where there are some personalities that rub other personalities the wrong way, so it is in the afterlife. It doesn't happen as frequently here because we tend to attract to ourselves only those who are of like mind or are aligned with our frequency.

Even so, there are other entities that pass through our dimension on the way to somewhere else, and we quickly learn we don't have to interact with them—or even to acknowledge them—as they are passing through.

For instance, there might be entities passing through from other dimensions who have a completely different view of reality from ours. They might be exploring our reality just for the fun of it or out of curiosity. If we were to blend with them, they might bring us a perception or an attribute, which could be harmful for us and could hinder us from manipulating our own environment.

I suppose you could use the example of interspecies mating as an analogy. If you cross a horse with a dog, you might get a hard working, loyal new species. On the other hand, such a mating might also result in a ferocious, snarling beast that would just as soon stomp on you as snap at you with its teeth.

In other words, some combinations might not be useful or expedient for either participant in its present state of evolution. Here, this is more apparent to us than it might be to you, for we have the ability to "see right through" other beings and to know everything about them just from coming near to them.

Now, I'm not saying such combinations won't happen at some point within the overall scheme of the universe, for I have said that, within the concept of God-All-That-Is, there is the concept of all aspects being combined into one whole unit.

Perhaps a better way for me to explain this would be to use the analogy of baking a cake. If you bake a cake from scratch, you have certain ingredients you combine. You have your wet ingredients, such as eggs, shortening, water, and flavorings. Then you have your dry ingredients, such as flour and sugar. To obtain the best results, you combine the wet ingredients together and you combine the dry ingredients together. Then you mix the two combinations together, whip in a certain volume of air, pour the blended mixture into a pan, and put it into the oven to bake.

You would have a disaster on your hands if you were to take the eggs and water, throw them into the pan, put them into the oven for a period of time, and then try to mix in the flour and sugar. Most likely, the combination of the heat and the eggs would give you scrambled eggs, and adding the dry ingredients to the eggs would give you not cake, but floury, sugary, scrambled eggs.

Thus when we are blending with each other here, we are following a recipe. It is not necessarily a recipe we are consciously aware of, but it is a recipe nonetheless. There is an intuitive part of ourselves that knows what to do and what not to do. But it certainly gives new meaning to the expression, "You can be anything you want to be," wouldn't you say?

You must also remember, I am not limited by your concepts of time and space anymore. It's all right here. It's all right now. I can be any part of it or all of it. There are no limits.

One of the key changes occurring in my perception is that I'm losing the concept of individuality. When I first arrived here, I still thought of myself as an individual personality. When I gathered together with other beings, I perceived them as separate beings. But now I'm seeing the boundaries between "myself" and "other beings" as less meaningful.

You have to admit, on earth, when you have an outside surface of a solid body that you can call your own, and you can feel other bodies and recognize them as "not you," the idea of individuality and numerical quantities makes sense. But, here, when we keep becoming less and less solid, when we can change shape and form at will, when we can appear or disappear, when we can blend with another so that the idea of "me" and "not me" are both the same, then individuality starts to seem very strange indeed.

All in all, my concept of "self" is much less distinct than it was on earth. I can be me or not me. I can be an individual or a group. I can be all that is or nothing at all. I can be all these concepts or none of them. Or something else entirely.

Chapter Thirteen

What's There To Do Here?

*S*ooner or later everyone who arrives in the afterlife from a lifetime on earth gets around to asking one simple question: "What's there to do here?" And the answer is almost as simple: "Anything you want."

When I first came here from my deathbed, all I wanted to do was jump and dance and shout because I was so happy to be rid of my cancer-ridden body and to be free from the pain. The dancing and jumping were such pleasures after being confined to my bed for many weeks before I made the final journey off the earth. But soon I wanted to know what else there was to do. I found life here in the afterlife has many of the same elements as life on earth. That is, we play, we work, and we go to school.

When we arrive in the afterlife, our first task is to create a lifestyle for ourselves. While we are free to use our imagination, many of us feel more comfortable at first creating a lifestyle that is familiar, a lifestyle resembling the one we just left behind. Having strong memories of our most immediate past earth life, we use these memories to help determine how well we are manifesting our thoughts into concrete reality.

At first we undergo training in what I'll call "creation skills." Many people first arriving here may not have realized they were creating everything in their just-finished physical lifetime. So now they will be shown how the creation process works. They will be given instruction on taking thoughts and ideas and forming them into events and objects. Such skills come in handy in the afterlife, as they do on earth.

After we have adopted the body we want, we set about to create our living quarters and other objects we believe we must have to "live" comfortably. For example, many of us will create automobiles or other vehicles to transport ourselves, and we will create roads, highways, and city streets to drive around on.

Also, there will be merchants who will set up stores to sell to others. There will be shopping activities and other forms of commerce similar to that on earth. We may even continue to eat food and engage in other activities familiar to us on earth. There is even an economy here. We will use money for a time to buy merchandise in our stores because it feels more familiar and comfortable.

Everyone is prosperous in the afterlife; there are no poor or homeless beings here. For some reason, everybody seems to come into this realm with an inherent knowledge that we are well provided for and that we have access to all the abundance and wealth that we desire. Some will be quite content with simpler lives and "middle class" standards while others find great joy in becoming extremely wealthy. But I have not observed anyone you could say was truly poor. They apparently subscribe to that old saying, "I've been rich and I've been poor, and rich is better."

Playing with money and prosperity is only temporary, however. It is apparently only a training program established to allow us to realize we have access to unlimited wealth and abundance. After a while we realize we are creating it all ourselves anyway. Hence we conclude we no longer need money to buy things; we can simply create the things we desire. From then on we stop "buying" things and start "making" things with our own thoughts and desires.

There are some who like to recreate earth-like scenery to play in. For example, they might build a mountain, design some challenging ski slopes, add some beautiful white snow, and go skiing. They will then play with the idea of speeding down the slopes with the wind in their faces, the snow kicking up behind their skis, and the air a bit nippy. The only thing missing will be the physical pain if they take a tumble, for here we do not feel extreme physical sensations such as pain.

Someone else might design a beautiful beach in order to lie on the sand on a summer day, listening to the waves pounding on the shore, the sea gulls squawking above, and the sea breezes blowing ever so softly, ever so gently.

There will be times when we will be called on to participate in someone else's fantasy, if you will. For example, someone might want to know what it feels like to be an airline pilot on a flight from New York to Los Angeles with two hundred passengers aboard. That person will express a desire for others to participate in the fantasy. Everyone who is interested will then come together, build a group reality of La Guardia Airport with airplanes, runways, luggage, and everything else they need. They will then play out the fantasy together until their plane lands at Los Angeles International Airport, at which point they will all turn to each other and say, "That was a lot of fun!" and end the scene, each participant flickering out and going its separate way once more.

Even more fun is a group of people who want to know what it feels like to be a tall tree standing in a forest. Everyone who has the same curiosity will come together, form a forest, stand around and experience it for a while, then flicker out of the scene, saying "Hey! That was far out!" "Why don't we all go out and be a flock of birds the next time?" "Yeah, what a great idea!"

Why would anyone create such earth-like scenes? Perhaps they want to remember their favorite activities when they were living in physical bodies. Others may never have had the opportunity in their lifetimes to have taken a ski trip or to go to the seashore. Thus they will create such adventures for themselves here, since they have all the time they desire to play.

When we create such earth-like attributes as weather, economies, social structures, cities and towns, living quarters, cars, and even our solid bodies covered by clothing of various fashions, we know these things are not "real." In other words, we know we are creating these things for our own entertainment and comfort. Unlike most human beings on earth, we are aware that we are creating our reality from moment to moment.

As we reach this level of understanding and become adept at creating our environment and all the things in it, we soon realize that it is much more efficient to create in a less dense arena. Hence we move gradually from solid to non-solid states of being. All of this is just a matter of moving our consciousness from one vibratory frequency to another vibratory frequency. When we have become acclimated to states of consciousness at higher frequencies (and less density), we move on to states of being where there is no solid matter at all.

You could think of this more "solid" level of the afterlife as a way station to provide a transition for us until we become acclimated to living at higher frequencies and manipulating in less dense environments. Gradually, as we go on about our living here, and as we evolve to new states of consciousness, the molecular structure we have created for ourselves will break down or transmute into less solid forms.

At some point we will give up our previous habit of eating, since food is not truly necessary to keep our bodies alive in the nonphysical realms of the afterlife. We will also give up our vehicles when we learn to transport ourselves from one place to another by our own thought. Finally, our bodies will become less solid and less "formed." In other words, our bodies will become more transparent and etheric. As our bodies become less solid, we find even more fun things to do. In fact, I believe the most fun can be had in the least dense environments. Thus there is an incentive to keep evolving in the afterlife.

How rapidly does all of this occur? It varies for each individual personality. Some may stay in this realm in a solid state for many thousands of years in your time frame. For others it is a short transitory period until they are ready to move on and explore other realms. Many, if not most, will choose to stay in the more solid realms of the afterlife until they are ready to go back once again into lifetimes on earth. They believe they will be able to acclimate to the conditions of their new lives if they maintain a reality system still closely aligned with that found in the physical realms of earth.

There are also some who migrate into these realms from other reality systems to obtain some training in the use of physical consciousness before going on to be born on earth for the first time. The more experienced here will then assist in the training of the newcomers, showing them what they need to know about physical reality and giving them tips, tricks, and traps to watch out for.

We also work here in the afterlife. When I say "work," I don't mean drudgery, for we left drudgery behind when we left the earth with all its rules about having to work hard in order to deserve to take up space on the planet. Nor do I mean what we do for money, because we don't have to have money to live here. All is taken care of and there is no sense of having to work for our keep.

What I mean by "work" here is activity to which we like to devote our primary energy: that which gives us the most meaning for ourselves and that which we believe will enhance us in the greatest manner possible. On the other hand, once we have chosen something to do, there is nothing to stop us from changing our minds and doing something else soon after.

I have thought about practicing law here, and I do still keep my hand in it, especially when lawyers on earth call on me for assistance. The way this works is someone will ask for help, or they might send a prayer to the universe at large. Their prayer will carry with it a specific vibratory frequency. Anyone who has the solution to their problem will tune in to the same vibratory frequency and will respond.

It is not necessary for us to know the person we are assisting, for we realize we are all one consciousness anyway. The assistance will be offered freely and with love. The person on the receiving end will obtain the assistance in the form of a flash of insight, or perhaps a dream, or they will just "know" what to do next.

Much of what you call "intuition" is someone in the afterlife feeding you the information you need. Therefore if you want to increase your intuition, or even lighten the burden of your daily living, just start asking us for help.

There are vast groups here in the afterlife who love to assist their fellow human beings on earth in their work or with their day-to-day living. For any occupation you can think of, there are beings here who can and do help. If they had meaningful careers on earth, they may wish to continue this work in the afterlife. For example, many scientists may set up laboratories and continue their research. Instead of publishing their findings in the media, as they would have on earth, they will align themselves with scientists on earth and inspire those scientists to create the same experiments.

It does not matter how long the person in the afterlife has been "dead" or how advanced the technology might have become on earth. There is still all the assistance you need. We have our own scientists and technical gurus who are advancing the knowledge and inspiring the advancement of technology on earth. We also have people who are leaving the earth every day and bringing their knowledge of the latest technologies with them. We then blend with their energy and we are all brought up to date.

I am also doing other things here that you could call my work. First, I am associating with others to learn all I can about the workings of the universe and to convey my knowledge to still others. I am also studying the nature of the spirit realms so that I can move to higher levels of consciousness. In other words, I am seeking to grow and evolve in the spiritual quest I embarked on when I came here. I do this mostly in the form of studying in groups. You might say I am going to college and taking yet another advanced degree. The difference, however, is that I am also exploring the universe on my own and contributing my own findings to the pool of knowledge. In other words, not only am I a student, but I am also becoming a teacher.

I have been spending some of my time, as well, welcoming newcomers into the afterlife. If you will remember, when I was first moving my own consciousness into these realms, I noticed there were beings who came to greet me and to make me feel welcome and comfortable. They looked after me and made sure I did not fall into fear or panic when I was encountering unfamiliar situations. I greatly appreciated the attention they paid to me and saw the importance of these orientation committees.

There are some in these realms who are working as guides and guardians for people who are presently incarnated on earth. When the time is right, they will then welcome their "soul mates" home to the afterlife and then take their turn on earth, giving their soul mates a chance to become their guides.

Because we do not have to spend a third of our time asleep, as you do, we find we can accomplish much more here. But I do not want to give you the impression it is all work and no play here, for that is simply not true. We don't have structured work hours here. Everything here is completely spontaneous. When I feel like working, I decide what I want to do, and the next thing I know, I flicker into a scene in which I find myself working. If I want to then take off and go to the beach, for example, I need only to think about it, and then I'm immediately transported to the beach.

On earth, to take off on a moment's notice and go to the beach would have meant instant termination of one's job. Here, on the other hand, we are all constantly doing what we want to do in any given moment, whether "working" or "playing." No matter what we decide to do, that is the most appropriate thing we can be doing. Everything is in perfect balance at all times.

Your lives on earth could be much more balanced as well. But you get out of balance often because you have made all these rules about what you should or should not be doing at any given moment. It seems as if you're always doing something way down on your list of priorities. In other words, you're sitting in your office working on some project, but you really want to be down at the beach. Or you may be lying on the beach, but then you'll find yourself thinking about all the things you need to do at the office. It seems as though you're never doing exactly what you want to be doing. While you're doing any particular thing, you're always thinking about doing something else in that moment.

I have also been continuing to learn and to explore here. I continue to take classes in order to improve my skills in manipulating in this nonphysical environment. Here, instead of parents and siblings to set the framework for our socialization, we have teachers and students. We have many teachers here in the afterlife. Any time we have a question or want to explore something, we can invite them forward.

You have a similar phenomenon going on in your online computer networks. You can log on to one of your online networks, enter a particular "forum," ask your question, and, lo and behold, you find someone else replying to your question. You don't know someone is there until they send a message back to you. You don't even have to see the person. The answer is all that counts.

In the afterlife the old maxim, "When the student asks, the teacher appears," is the rule. I may be going along creating or playing or just lounging around not doing much of anything, when all of a sudden I will ponder: "I wonder how this works." "Gee, how does that happen?" "I'm curious about those beings over there. Who are they and how do they relate to me?" Just bringing up the question in my mind emits a vibratory frequency that attracts the answer.

Sometimes the answer comes forward in the form of a teacher who appears out of nowhere to sit down with me and explain all I want to know. When I feel satisfied and complete, the teacher disappears. Other times I will find myself flickering off from the scene and flickering back on in another scene where there is a classroom going on and they are discussing the question I just raised. Still other times I can find myself in a library and I'm reading all about it in some book. Sometimes I stay right where I am and the answer comes to me without the appearance of a teacher or the change of scenery. It just comes to me as knowledge.

Perhaps there will be more than myself wanting to learn some particular thing. We will then be drawn to each other, and the teacher will be drawn to our group. We will most likely find ourselves in a classroom setting, if that is the most appropriate forum in which to learn.

We have wonderful institutions of learning here that look like your college campuses. I'm told that your colleges and universities have been designed after our institutions. The institution I find myself in most often is a campus traditional in its architecture. Not only are there large buildings with great auditoriums, but also there are classrooms for small groups to sit around a conference table in a seminar approach to learning. Sometimes we will sit together as a group outside under a beautiful tree. It all depends on what we desire and what seems most appropriate.

Oftentimes—and perhaps this is even most of the time—we meet with our teachers one-on-one. We might take a stroll together through a beautiful pastoral scene, or we might walk along a beach. Other times we may find ourselves sitting together in a furnished room.

The "scene" in which we do our learning is all a product of our own imagination. If I feel comfortable in a one-on-one setting with my teacher, that will be what I will create. But others may be there as well that I don't see, yet they may be aware of me and of each other. Thus while I am seeing a twosome in a sitting room, they may be placing the same scene in a large lecture hall on a college campus. Moreover, the same teacher may be working with us in both scenes simultaneously. Or to take this even further, the teacher may have created still another scene, say, under a tree outside. In all these scenes we are still connected to each other and to the teacher, and we are all absorbing the same information.

In your world you have mandatory formal education where you find yourself spending the first part of your life being trained by others who are older and more experienced than you. You are often being taught subjects others have chosen for you to learn, whether you want to learn those subjects or not. You also have created in your society educational systems whereby a group of you will progress through a series of levels at a standardized rate until your entire cohort is educated.

After your mandatory childhood education is completed, you may pursue further academic or vocational training, as well as to engage in more frivolous pursuits in your adult education field. You may take seminars and workshops from teachers who advertise their services, and you may hire individual teachers for tutoring in specific subjects of interest to you. You also have a cadre of inner teachers who are with you throughout your life, who wait for you to acknowledge them and ask for their help or who work with you in your sleep.

As I've already indicated, we have both our visible and our invisible teachers here, just as you do there. Perhaps we're more aware of our unseen teachers than you are of yours. When we ask a question or ponder something in our mind and the answer comes back to us, we know we are interacting with a teacher who has been drawn to us. It happens instantaneously.

It's rather amazing when you stop to think about it. Any thought we could ever have instantly connects with similar thoughts throughout the vastness of this infinite universe and attracts its answer instantly. Can you see how powerful that is? It means we can ask any question and we will receive the answer instantly. Thus we can say we are all-knowing because the answer to any question is immediately available to us just for the asking.

That's another major difference between our educational system here and your educational system on earth. You believe all the answers to your questions are not in your power to have. You learn this in school as a child when you ask questions and the teachers tell you that you have to wait until the proper grade to learn the answer or to study that topic. Or your parents tell you that you're not yet old enough to know the answer. By the time you reach adulthood, you have been indoctrinated to believe you cannot know anything unless there is a formal system to teach it to you. This formality leads you to believe the learning of anything is just plain hard work, and probably not worth the effort in most cases. So you stop learning and you stop asking questions.

Most of all, you believe you can't possibly know everything there is to know. Here we believe otherwise. Here we realize knowledge is available for the asking and it is freely given to anyone who seeks it. Since knowledge is very easily obtained, we spend more time learning on this side of the veil than you do on your side.

So you ask me, what do I do all day (and all night, for that matter, because we don't have physical bodies that have to be put to sleep)? And my answer to you is, "I learn." It's as simple as that. I learn.

Chapter Fourteen

Creating Our Own Outer World

My world is more closely akin to a dream state. In other words, I find myself in scenes, and then I flicker off from one scene and flicker on in another scene. But I don't necessarily touch the objects in the scene I'm in. I no longer create a physical body that can go bumping into walls, nor do I stub my toes on the furniture. But I can move my body around. I can also create a scene where I am sitting on a chair, for instance, and the chair is holding me up. I can be looking at a wall, for example, and I can make the wall look "solid"—that is, in the sense of opaque instead of transparent—so that I cannot see through the wall. And I suppose I could create a scene where I would go right up and bump my nose against the wall, but there would be no sensation of physical touch or pain or a bloody nose. Well, maybe I could create the bloody nose if I wanted to.

The point is that the afterlife is more of a mental world than a physical world. That is, it is a concept we form with our thoughts, beliefs, and imagination, just as you form your dream world. I'm creating it all with my consciousness. As soon as I stop desiring to create one scene or situation, I then can move instantly to create another scene or situation. In other words, it's all like lucid dreaming. I'm very conscious of what I'm doing with my consciousness as I'm doing it.

But there are some differences too. For one thing, your dream state carries more of a story line than does my reality here. You focus your attention on linear progressions through time and space, and you recreate the same perception in your dream state. That is, you have more of a "plot" in your dreams than I have in my world.

In the afterlife I'm getting away from the idea of movement through space or movement through time periods. Instead my perception is more of moving into greater intensity or lesser intensity.

You have heard that your thoughts create your reality. Yet many of you forget that in your everyday living. One reason you forget is that you are focusing your attention most of the time in the reality you have already created, your so-called outer world with its solid "props" that you perceive with your three-dimensional eyesight.

When you are sitting within the environment you have created for yourself in your outer world, you forget that you created your environment with your thoughts because it seems to stay in place when you leave it, and it will be there exactly as you remembered it when you return. You don't realize your memory of your outer world is constantly recreating itself just as you remembered it. Yet if you were to go away from your usual "scenery" for a period of time and then return to it much later, say, after a period of years, you would then see it with different eyes. That is, it would look different from the way you remembered it.

Many of you who go back to find your childhood home comment that it looks different from the way you remembered it. That is because solid items in your dense outer world have a tendency to maintain their vibratory frequency long after you yourself have moved on to new frequencies with your thoughts. In returning, you recreate in your memory a new perspective and then are surprised when you see the "real" thing.

One of the major differences between our nonphysical realm and your physical realm is that you cannot live in your physical realm without a solid body. If you could, what would be the point? You live in a reality system that has its whole basis in density. Your thoughts create matter you interpret as solid objects, providing both the subject matter and the object matter, not to mention the backdrop, of your life.

You are like a painter and a sculptor. You paint a scene with your mind, as an artist might paint a scene on canvas. Then you go one step further and make your painting three-dimensional so that you can walk right into it and be surrounded by it. You then become a sculptor and create solid objects in the foreground you can walk around and among. You may then pick up some of these objects and use them for other activities you create as you go along. Finally, you create other life forms—people, animals, and plants—so that you can have some interaction with other conscious beings. These all fill up your environment and allow you to create dramas that you call the events of your life. You also create other accompaniments to enhance your "painting," such as sounds you can hear, temperature gradients you can feel, smells. . . . Well, you get the idea.

And let's not forget your own body, which you are also creating moment by moment as you go along. Your body is a most useful vehicle because it allows you to stand up and walk around in the scenery you have just created. Or you can lie down or sit down or get into still other vehicles such as your car to explore your scenery. This adds even more depth and variety to the drama you are creating. In a nutshell, this is your "life" and you are creating it all from moment to moment.

Here in the nonphysical realms of the afterlife, we also paint scenes and walk into them. But we are not limited to the creation of solid objects. You might say we have more media to use in the creation of our outer world. These media can be either solid or non-solid. We can duplicate your earth-like environment or we can experiment with environments completely foreign to your conceptualization.

Without a solid physical body to lug around, there is truly no necessity to have a solid background scenery to place it in. Still, we continue to create scenery as a backdrop to whatever we find ourselves doing, although even that is truly not necessary. The scenery can be just as "real" as that which adorns your outer world. That is to say, we can be surrounded with as much or as little detail as we choose.

You experience pretty much the same phenomenon in your own world. There are times when you are very cognizant of your outer world scenery, and you notice every minute detail. At other times you are focused on particular objects or people, and you are not paying attention to the background at all. At those times the background tends to fade away into a blur. Sometimes you can become so focused on a particular person or thing that you do not notice the background at all and would not be able to remember anything about it later.

This is similar to what happens in our world. We paint a backdrop when desirable or necessary. At other times we become focused on what we are doing with our companions of the moment, and we do not pay attention to the background. For all we know, we could be suspended in a vacuum. In fact, there are many times when I will be talking to someone, and then I will notice we are both just suspended in a background of white (or sometimes black) nothingness. The other person then appears as an almost translucent hologram projecting out of nothingness. Yet our conversation and inter-action seems just as "real" as if we had created a solid earth-like scene complete with ground, sky, and everything in between.

I find this whole concept fascinating here, and so I am having a lot of fun playing with these ideas. It is extremely creative. Who would have thought you could create your "life" by painting a picture and then moving right into the picture you've just created?

You may be wondering if we have a sky, sun, moon, planets, stars, and such. The answer is quite simple. Each of us is at the center of our own universe and we can fill it with anything we desire. Hence some will build a universe looking very much like the earth with a moon, sun, blue sky, white puffy clouds, birds flying by, or whatever else they would like to create in their scene. Some will also create the nighttime periodically so that they can wander outside and look up at the beautiful dark sky with the moon, the Big Dipper, and the Milky Way.

Some of us will place ourselves in a plain scene and will allow the background to—well, fade away into the background. We will then place objects or beings in our scene that will be clearly in focus in the foreground. In this case we desire to have a less cluttered look and want to maintain our focus on those objects or beings we have placed in our foreground without being distracted by the background.

Our world is not as rigidly defined as your world. You have certain commonly held beliefs about your physical environment, and you train yourselves to perceive your world according to the rules that have been set up for you. For example, you believe the sky is blue, the grass is green, the clouds are white or various shades of gray. You do not go around perceiving the sky to be chartreuse, the clouds to be bright orange, or the grass to be purple. In our world we can and do create our scenes in any of these colors and more. It is fun to play with these ideas and concepts when we first arrive here. It brings out the creativity in us and it is playful and exciting.

Moreover, our perceptions don't have to be shared by others. For example, I can be standing here with two others in the same scene, and we might all view it differently. I might have painted the scene of my garden, and I might have placed my two friends in chairs and have us all drinking lemonade and eating cookies. At the same time my friend, A, might place us at the beach sitting on the sand and watching the waves come in. My friend, C, might have us all standing atop a tall skyscraper looking out over the city at sunset, only the sun is green, not orange. Yet we are all three having a conversation "together."

On the other hand, I might be walking along and decide to join my friend, B, who has already created a scene for herself, and I can join her in the scene she has created. I do this by tuning in on the same wavelength to which she is tuned, then I will see her scene. But then I might think of something else or some place else while I am still together with my friend, B, and then she will tune in on my scene and see it as I am seeing it. This is all a lot of fun, to see what others are creating and to share with them what I am creating.

All of this, of course, is because we create everything in our outer world from our thoughts, and we know we are doing it. Or if we don't know, we soon find out after we arrive here. In other words, what we believe or desire to create is what we create for ourselves. It's all in our own imagination, and no one's imagination is any more valid than anyone else's imagination. There is no such thing as "the truth" here. It's *all* the truth. The truth can be whatever we want it to be.

What we do here is not that different from what you do with respect to your outer world. But most of you do not realize your outer world is just a creation emanating from your mind. You think the moon, planets, stars, and galaxies are all real because you look out at your night sky and you see them there. They were there before you went outside, and they will continue to be there after you come back inside. But they are only real because someone told you they are real, and you believed what you were told.

Scientists will tell you those objects are real because they have looked at those objects with telescopes and other instruments. They have sent rocket ships with all kinds of sophisticated instrumentation to take measurements, gather data, and transmit the data back for analysis. "Of course, Mars is real. Didn't we land a vehicle there to take pictures? Didn't we send astronauts to the moon to gather up soil samples? There you have it. We have the cold, hard evidence."

But I submit to you, before the scientists sent their measuring devices out to analyze and to prove the existence of those heavenly bodies, someone had already created those objects in their mind. Over the course of centuries you refined your thinking about those heavenly bodies. If you will look through your history books, you will see your ideas about what is up there in your skies has changed, and changed and changed and changed. Right now, as you are reading these words, there are great thinkers who are hypothesizing other aspects of the physical universe and how those phenomena might be proved to be real and be measured.

It has only been a few years since scientists began to believe the galaxies in the physical universe are not evenly spaced apart or randomly scattered, but are situated in clusters. Sooner or later, someone will come up with a good explanation, and then someone else will go about designing instrumentation to measure it and prove it to be true. Then you will all adopt a new paradigm about your heavens based on what the scientists have reported to you. Children will learn about it in school, and they will form a different picture in their minds about their outer world.

This is going on every day in your world. As consciousness expands, it imagines new ideas. These ideas and thoughts inspire the scientists to design experiments to test them, and after they prove them to be "true," your knowledge expands once more. But it is all just imagination. You are making it all up.

As I said before, the only difference between your world and mine is I know mine is made up. I can play with changing it at the slightest whim. And then changing it again. And again. And again and again and again. In your world you have matter that is solid, so you cannot change your constructs as rapidly. Nevertheless your constructs are changing gradually over time.

If the skies and the planets and the stars and the galaxies are all just a product of your mind, then you must be wondering if we, too, have those constructs in the afterlife. And I do have to say that there are many of us who do, for we are still very much tied to the human condition and to human beliefs. Moreover, we have an advantage over your scientists because we are not constrained by technology to go exploring the physical universe.

On earth you have what is called a consensus reality system. That is, you are a part of a conscious mass known as the human consciousness, which has consistent ideas and beliefs about your experiences as human beings. You each have a similar perceptual apparatus and you thus perceive your outside world in a similar manner.

For example, you can go outside in a rainstorm and you can feel the rain falling on your skin. Temperature sensors in your skin examine the vibratory frequency range you know as hot and cold, and your mind creates an interpretation of its temperature. You can look up at the cloudy sky and see the rain clouds in various shades of gray. You might also see lightning and hear thunder, or you might hear the wind whistling through the trees. Ten of you standing together will all agree you are outside in a rainstorm because you have all been taught by your parents or teachers early in your life that what you are experiencing is a rainstorm.

Admittedly, there would be differences in your perceptions if we were to examine each one of you more closely about your experience of the rainstorm. For example, some of you might interpret the temperature as more or less cold than others. Some of you might see the clouds as brighter or darker than others. Some of you might associate this rainstorm with other experiences and form judgments about the rainstorm based on those other experiences.

For instance, a rainstorm to some of you might bring up memories of pleasant summer afternoon showers and opportunities to go splashing around in the puddles. Others might interpret the experience as a great inconvenience, especially if they are trying to keep dry. Thus even though you will all have a consensus about your rainstorm, each of you will also have a unique perspective based on an accumulation of past experiences as well as judgments absorbed by you from others that you believe and in whom you trust. So while you are all having the "same" experience, each of you is also having a unique experience. There is one consensus reality and there are ten individual realities simultaneously.

Here in the afterlife, we too have a simultaneous consensus reality with individual reality systems. But in our case we are focused more on the unique reality systems than on the consensus reality system. The reason for this is that we know our consciousness is actively creating our reality system even as we are experiencing it. Therefore we know we are the unique designers of our outer world.

On the other hand, we also realize we are all truly one consciousness, just as your ocean is one body of water. Any single aspect of this one consciousness (or, in our ocean analogy, any single molecule of water) can focus on its unique perspective, or it can see itself within the framework of its larger perspective as a region or even the entire ocean.

Going further, we can even experience our reality from two or more perspectives at once. I can focus my attention here or there, or both, or everywhere at once. I can view the reality of my own self, or I can blend in with the essence of others and gain a larger perspective of my reality. I can take my consciousness and stretch it out as far as I desire in order to see just how big it can become. Theoretically, I can go all the way to infinity and experience myself as God-All-That-Is and experience all that is as a reality system.

In practical terms, however, I cannot. For if I were to truly expand my consciousness that far, I would soon get lost in the vastness of it all. Very quickly it would become too much for me to comprehend and it would all become meaningless. In trying to ascribe meaning to the meaningless, my consciousness would see it as nothing.

Hence I can only perceive that to which I can attach meaning, and then a little bit more. But if I expand too far, I move into the strange unknown and then into nothingness. Even in that nothingness though, I realize the nothingness truly is something. I just can't perceive it with my conscious understanding. The essence of all of this is that we are all expanding our consciousness bit by bit, moving out beyond the boundaries.

PART IV

NEW PERSPECTIVES
ON LIFE

Chapter Fifteen

Forming New Concepts of the Universe

*Y*ou may be wondering how I perceive your world since I don't have a physical body and physical senses anymore. I perceive your world similar to the way you perceive mine. That is, I connect with your energy as though I were tuning in to a specific vibratory frequency. That particular frequency is then interpreted by my mind and creates a picture of you and your surroundings.

You start the process when you focus on your surroundings. That which surrounds you in your outer world is truly just a creation of your mind, which is focusing on a particular vibratory frequency in a band of infinite frequencies. As you focus on your outer world, you are then projecting that frequency out into the universe where anyone else can tune in to it. They will then perceive that energy and interpret it in symbology familiar to them.

Because I have recently departed from a lifetime as a human being within the same time and space dimensions as you, I can perceive your thoughts and draw on my memory, creating a picture in my own mind similar to the scene or situation you are creating with your thoughts. If I personally knew you during my lifetime as Susan Wells, I can imagine the two of us sitting together having a conversation, and I will draw on my memory of you as you appeared to me during my life in order to "see" you.

On the other hand, I may have never personally known you or visited your house during my lifetime as Susan Wells. Therefore my mental picture of you sitting in your living room will not be the same scene you see. If I had seen your house, then I could rely on my memory and imagine the scene much as it truly is. Either way, it doesn't matter what you or your surroundings look like, for your surroundings are merely your own creation anyway. What is important is the communication between us, not the body or the outer scenery in which we place ourselves.

You experience the same phenomenon in your own world when you, for example, talk on the telephone with someone. If you have previously seen them and their surroundings, you will visualize them and their surroundings based on your memory. But if you have no memory to rely on, you will still visualize both the person and their surroundings in your mind, and it truly does not matter if your visualization is "correct."

Going a step further, someone else who happens by and tunes into your broadcast of energy might interpret that energy quite differently if they had never been a human being. They would take your point of reference and translate it into something having meaning for themselves, using senses or methods of perception they have developed in their own realm. Their sensory perceptions might have nothing to do with your senses of sight, sound, taste, smell, or touch.

The process is not different from the process you use when you create a painting on canvas. You first tune in on a particular vibratory frequency in your inner self, receive a picture in your mind, and transcribe that picture into your outer world by brushing paint onto your canvas. If you are creating music you do the same thing. You start hearing a tune playing inside your mind. That tune is actually being broadcast by All-That-Is, and you are tuning in to it with your psyche. You then play the tune you hear on your musical instrument. Sometimes you are also editing as you go along, trying to make the picture or the music or the prose in your outer world match what you are receiving in your inner world. This is the creativity process in a nutshell.

What fascinates me is how simple it all is. With slight variations, it is the same across almost any endeavor you can think of, be it writing a book or inventing a gizmo.

But the mind-boggling part is that the source from which you are pulling your prose or your song or your painting or your invention is infinite. Moreover, your pulling out of your ideas is unique. While all beings in all times and all places (or even outside of space and time, for that matter) have access to the same source as you, no one will pull out exactly the same ideas as you will pull out. In other words, it appears that each of us has our own unique supply of resources, yet we are all drawing on the same source.

If you think for a moment about all the billions of people living on earth at this time alone, and think about all the people who have ever lived on earth, or will ever live on earth in the future, and then if you multiply that by all the planets in the entire universe, you will begin to have an idea how large this consciousness is. Yet it is all one consciousness that we are each tapping into, permitting each of us to connect with each other.

These ideas quickly fry the brain, which is why you seldom think about them, or if you do, not for long while you are in a physical body. But here in the afterlife, where we have no physical bodies to worry about, we contemplate these ideas often.

The homecoming into the nonphysical realms of the afterlife was a special event for me. It was a celebration of the return of my full conscious awareness back home from whence I had sprung forward to the earth to play out my lifetime as Susan Wells. But now that I am back home again, I realize I never truly left home at all, or at least not *all* of me. You see, when we are living a lifetime on earth, we are only focusing a small part of our consciousness on that endeavor while the rest stays here in the afterlife to oversee the production of the drama we are creating on earth. William Shakespeare once wrote, "All the world's a stage, and all the men and women merely players." What we are doing is putting on a play for the benefit of ourselves and those in our group consciousness to watch, to be entertained, and from which to learn valuable lessons.

Thus while I was moving through my lifetime, from the time I was born until the time I died, I was merely playing a role. My whole life was a series of episodes all asking these simple questions: "I wonder what will happen if I do this? I wonder what will happen if I do that?" From these episodes we produce with our lives, we then provide ourselves with insight into the workings of life on earth.

This is truly no different from the arts in which you have your movies, theater productions, operas, books, and television programs. All are giving you insight into the human experience. And not just human experience, I might add, for you have nature documentaries showing you how animals and plants live as well.

What was fascinating to me about this whole process, however, was that I was not only entertaining and enlightening my group with the events of my lifetime as I remember it, but I was also giving them a full rounded multidimensional production. By this I mean, at each turn I took in the road, I made a choice and focused my attention on the choice I had made. But from the perspective of the afterlife, both choices were visible and could be viewed, either in sequence, or simultaneously. Thus every probable outcome of every event in my lifetime as Susan Wells became a gigantic movie for myself and others to watch.

If you then realize everybody on the planet is also producing a life "movie," and if they are spinning off hundreds or thousands of versions of their lifetimes as they take the probable pathways along the way, you can begin to comprehend the vastness of this universe that we call God-All-That-Is. I understand this "movie making" is going on all over the universe. Every element of God is creating a record of its experiences that others can then tap into and view.

Not only that, but the story here gets even wilder, if I have not yet succeeded in boggling your mind. Not only can we sit down and watch a movie of someone's life, but the movie we are "seeing" is a full scale three-dimensional movie with a 360-degree movie screen and total surround sound. In other words, when we watch such a life script, we actually put ourselves into the movie and can become the person who is living that lifetime.

Moreover, if we don't like the choices the other person made, we can then make our own choices and see what will happen next. In other words, each person's life is like virtual reality. Anyone else can check out that movie and slip into that lifetime to experience it too.

If you have followed me so far, you will soon realize all our lifetimes on earth are none other than a series of movies that we created. There's a movie for every being that ever has, is, or will occupy the planet. There is even a movie of the planet from the perspective of the planet itself. And there is a movie of each of the other planets in our solar system, as well as a movie of each of their occupants, and a movie of the sun, and of the galaxy, and of the cluster of which our galaxy is a part. . . . well, I suppose, all the way up to God-All-That-Is.

I can hear you exclaiming, "My gosh! That's a *lot* of movies! It would take forever to check them all out and watch them all!" Yeah! Right! Exactly! So now you have an idea of what eternity is all about.

And now you also have an idea of what God is. God is this gigantic consciousness aware of itself and exploring each aspect of itself, while each aspect goes about doing everything possible to do. Each of these infinite aspects of God is doing the same thing God is doing. We're each going around exploring ourselves and each other. But no matter how much we explore, there is always more to be explored. It never ends. It just keeps on going. On and on. Forever.

Chapter Sixteen

Ushering in the New
Millennium on Earth

*M*any of you believe this new millennium is going to bring about the end of the world. You look around you at the crime, violence, chaos, wars, pollution of your air and water, mass destruction of your nature world, breakdown of the family, schools, government, and other cherished institutions, and you wonder how your world can possibly survive. You read your books and watch your TV programs about ancient prophecies (and even some New Age prophecies) foretelling the destruction of continental land masses, nuclear annihilation, invasions from UFO's,

183

plagues, polar shifts, and, ultimately, Armageddon.

But did you ever consider, these "end of the world" fears may be no more than a reflection of your fear of your own death? If you believe your death is the end of life and the annihilation of yourself, is it any wonder you would project the same annihilation onto your world?

This book has suggested—and I am here to tell you from my own experience—death is not the end of life. It is simply a change in lifestyle. Accordingly, wouldn't that suggest the beginning of this new millennium will bring about, not the end of the world, but a change in lifestyle? Instead of your world coming to an end, what I see is the end of your current lifestyle that has been fraught with crime, violence, war, and a frightening distrust and isolation from other human beings, from nature, and from God.

For many years energy waves have been transmitted to the earth from higher levels of consciousness in the nonphysical realms. Some of you are feeling those waves of energy and are wondering what is the meaning of it all. What effect will there be going forward?

As I understand it, those energy waves are being transmitted in order to send shock waves to the earth to help bring about the end of the old lifestyle you have known and to usher in a new millennium on earth that will be rich with beauty, harmony, peace, and joy.

Many of you have been wondering what you might expect as you move forward into this new millennium. You will be happy to know you can expect a bit of relief from your worries and your fears, for many of you have been forced into situations in these past several years where you have had to let go of old habits, old patterns of thinking, old processes of living. You have had to clean house and get rid of those things that no longer serve you.

For many of you who resisted the letting go, you found you could no longer hang on anyway. Those things you tried to cling to were yanked away from you. Some of you lost your health, others lost relationships, and many of you lost all your money and financial security. In fact, if there was any pattern in all those losses, the losses all had to do with your ideas of security and self-identification. For those who identified themselves through their work and their careers, many lost their jobs. For others who believed financial wealth would make them feel safe, the proverbial rug was pulled out from under them. For still others who depended on significant relationships, they found those relationships falling away through separation, divorce, or death, sometimes quite abruptly.

In all cases you have been experiencing what it feels like to have old lifestyles and patterns of perception break down and fall away. But in each case you also have been given a beautiful opportunity to see for yourself *you* still survived even when you thought your whole life had fallen apart.

Many of you perceived—and correctly so— these old ways taken away from you were gifts from higher levels of your own consciousness to prepare you for a new and freer lifestyle, a lifestyle built on trust, a lifestyle that will be more spontaneous and joyful because you will no longer feel trapped by the limitations that in the past kept you locked in place. For some of you—perhaps most of you—this process has brought pain. But remember, pain is a beautiful gift which signals a healing is taking place, a healing that will leave you better off than before.

For some of you there will still be some cleaning up to do even after the new millennium rings in. But this cleaning up will feel good to you. You will see you have been set free, and you will be anxious to put away those last few people, situations, attitudes, or beliefs that no longer serve you.

Not everyone will feel this movement into the new millennium in exactly the same manner. Most of the human population may move through it unaware of what is taking place. It's as though they will sleep right through the ringing in of the New Millennium. But no matter. They will still be in the new consciousness and in the new vibratory frequency.

As you continue to move into higher states of consciousness, you will find more people waking up and setting themselves free from the old limitations. For those who readily give up their past and willingly change with the changing frequencies, they will enjoy smooth sailing. For others who resist the tides of change and try to hang on to their worries and their defeatist attitudes, they will experience even more pressure, just as your rocks experience a buildup of pressure before they snap loose in an earthquake.

You will start to notice more people around you letting go of old habits and beliefs that no longer serve them. They will then free themselves from the painful constrictions under which they have lived and feel a closer connection with their spiritual nature. Aligning with their spiritual nature will allow them to perceive their outer world in a new light. And, yes, that pun was fully intended. For, you see, the waves of energy bounding right through your planet and each of you have been adding light frequencies to counteract some of the darkness that has befallen the planet.

Going forward, you will see more and more attention paid to fostering world peace and world harmony. There will be much more compassion for the plights of Third World countries. There will be much less tolerance for old ways of settling the score by fighting and wars.

Many of you have been worried about holding together all the situations in your outer world, feeling as if you must do something to maintain control, to make something happen, or to prevent something else from happening. What you are all learning how to do right now is to float freely and to allow your life to unfold as it will. This is why you are being advised constantly to focus only on today and to not worry about what is going to happen tomorrow.

I can assure you, the pressure you have all been feeling is now about to ease up and you will not find yourselves struggling as hard. That is, if you will listen to this advice and relax. In other words, I'm advising you not to resist your life. Just let it happen and marvel at all you are experiencing. Try not to make judgments about what you are experiencing. Just remind yourself, "This is just another experience my Higher Self has given me to learn from." "Here is yet another experience my Higher Self has given me to learn from." And so on throughout your day.

If you see yourself sliding down the proverbial hill or even falling off the cliff, don't worry about what is going to happen next.

Just experience the fall. Just live it. I can assure you, every experience is the best possible experience you could be having in that particular moment. Good or bad, it doesn't matter. It is the perfect experience for you. Looking back on it later, you will realize you couldn't have created it any better if you had wanted to. Everything—and I mean *everything*—always turns out for the best. Just keep reminding yourself of that when you start down a path of worry, fright and depression.

In the first few years of the new millennium it will be even more important for you to bring balance into your individual life, for the energy all about you is going to be quite chaotic. If you don't stay centered in the core of your spiritual essence where you can maintain your connection with your inner source of strength, truth, and light, you are likely to go dashing into your outer world and get caught up in the drama and trauma all about you.

It is important for you to see the chaos in your outer world for what it truly represents: a mirror of your inner world. In the coming years you are going to see more clearly the connection between your inner thoughts, beliefs, and feelings and their manifestation as people, situations, and events in your outer world. You will no longer be able to ignore the connection, for it will be patently obvious when you have some thought in one moment and then you experience that thought as an event in the very next moment.

In the past many of you have felt as though you were marionettes in someone else's stage production. You have felt someone else in the background far above you and behind you pulling the strings to make you do what you were doing. You have felt as though you had no personal control over yourself or the events in your life. This is changing rapidly as many of you come to realize your strings have been cut and you are no longer being controlled by anyone but yourself. You now must go on with the production through your own volition, creating whatever steps you desire.

Many of you have made a giant leap in consciousness from one reality system to another. You may not feel it much right now because your outer world still appears the same. It is as though your new world and your old world are superimposed on each other. Therefore for many of you, you may still see the violence and the chaos in your outer world.

On the other hand, many of you are no longer emotionally attached to the violence and the chaos in your outer world. You say to yourself, "Oh, well, so there is still violence, crime, and negativity out in the world, and the news broadcasts are still just as negative as ever." But you are not experiencing that violence and crime in your own life. It is just on TV or in the newspapers. Many of you have come to realize the chaos and the negativity are in somebody else's backyard, not your own. And you are perfectly willing to let it be just as it is. You're saying to yourselves, "I know there is chaos, crime, violence and war in the world, but there is no longer such in *my* world. I have peace, contentment and serenity in my life. If others choose to experience crime and violence, or to be victims, then so be it. I no longer choose to live like that myself." Then you are going on about your business being peaceful and serene. You no longer believe you have to save the world, nor even the forests, nor even the whales.

As you continue to go on about your own business creating your own life, you will move further and further away from the reality of the tragedies and disasters. Soon you will begin to notice a difference in your media. You will think the broadcasters have changed their programming content: They have given up their emphasis on negativity and sen-sationalism, and they have started to focus their attention on the more positive aspects of living. But this will just be another one of your own creations. You will realize you are creating positive events in your own life, and so you will begin to believe others are doing the same for themselves. Because like attracts like, you will continue to move into a more peaceful world with other supportive, growth-oriented, loving beings just like yourself.

For some of you there will continue to be the temptation to go back to the old world and to try to rescue some who have been left behind. Each time you do this, however, you will fail in your attempt because everyone is just where he should be and wants to be. If other people wanted to be in your world instead of their own, they would be. If those people wanted peace and serenity instead of drama and trauma, they would have it.

There may be some who will see what you have and may want it for themselves. And there may even be some who will want you to stop what you are doing and give them what you have. If so, you are only reflecting your own beliefs that you must rescue and save others. You can choose at any time to stop rescuing others and start taking care of your own needs. You will then be able to put those needy hangers-on out of your life.

Do not feel guilty when you do so. Instead pat yourself on the back for taking care of yourself and honoring your own needs. Give others the gift of example. If you are honoring yourself and taking care of your own needs, then they will have an example to follow, especially if you don't stop what you are doing to go to their rescue. When there is no one to rescue them, they will then look to themselves for their own rescue, and they will have a growth opportunity you gave them by not rescuing them.

Soon you will find yourself in a world in which people take care of themselves and do not expect others to take care of them. The welfare system you have had in your society over the past century will fall away. People will take back their dignity, become self-empowered, and learn to take care of themselves.

I know it is tough for you right now as the energy waves accelerate around your planet and break up old patterns you have all held onto, patterns of energy that have given you structure and meaning in your lives. But this break up of old patterns is necessary to bring about the new patterns. Just think of this as the cold, gray days of December on your planet, when all the leaves have fallen off the trees, the skies are leaden, and everything seems bleak and dismal. You feel depressed by the darkness and dreariness of it all. But you know resistance will not do you any good, for the winter must have its time. Know that spring will follow in its own proper time, bringing about a new burst of life, a new burst of joy, a new burst of wonder and excitement. So let the old ways die. Allow yourself to suffer your pain and your discontent. I can assure you, it will all be worth it when the new energy bursts through like the first crocuses of spring.

I want you to realize, this wave of new energy is not just being opened to your human consciousness. It is of universal scope. You might say it is a birth of God-All-That-Is into a new state of being, for even God, the Creator of us all, is continually being born anew and awakens to new states of consciousness in its infinite state of becoming. Just as scientists are finding out your evolutionary processes don't always advance smoothly and steadily, but instead move forward in jumps and starts, so does this entire universe. The ushering in of the new millennium is another beautiful jump in the universal evolution.

I want to assure you, those of you who are pioneering in this new level of consciousness have only a short while longer to endure this feeling that you are out of synchronization with the rest of the world. A few of you are pulling the entire mass consciousness of the world to this new frequency, and you are feeling the strain of the pull, as though that mass consciousness were attached to you with a rubber band. Soon, there will be a major shift in which the entire mass consciousness will spring forward and reach the place to which you have pulled it. You will then feel you have come back into synchronization again.

For those of you who are doing the pulling, just remember, we are helping you and providing you the strength and the courage you need. If you are feeling exhausted by the struggle, remember that the pain you are going through is nothing more than the birth pangs of the new consciousness. When the going is rough, please ask for help. We will come forward immediately to assist and to ease your burden.

In a short time the veil between our realms will lift, and we will be able to perceive each other and to communicate with each other. What it is going to take is for enough of you to realize the blindness and deafness is on your side. There are a few of you who have already opened your eyes and ears to behold the wonder of which I speak. Each day in your time brings more and more human beings awake and aware. Soon—much sooner than you may realize—there will be enough of you who have shifted into this new state of awareness that the entire group conscious-ness of your world will come awake. There is a new day coming, my friends, and the dawning of this new day is as exciting for us as it is for you. Perhaps it is even more so for us. We are already aware of the brilliance and the beauty that is forthcoming.

We in the nonphysical realms of the afterlife are celebrating your growth. We are cheering you on. We feel the pain many of

you have been through these past few years,
and we kiss your psychic wounds and give
you a loving hug. We offer our assistance and
will always be at your side. Do remember
your life is a team work with your angels,
guides, and friends in the afterlife. When you
feel burdened, be sure to share your burden
with us.

We honor you for listening to us when we
share our creative ideas with you. We will
continue to keep our ideas coming your way
and will be thrilled beyond compare when you
pick up those ideas and run with them. We
will share your laughter, your joy and your
playfulness when you help us put our joint
creativity into form in your physical world.
And we stand in awe and marvel at the
beautiful creations we have made together.

This movement into the new millennium is
a beautiful opportunity for all of us to come
closer together as one, to laugh together, to
sing together, to create together, to bask in
our light and love together.

Looking forward to the ushering in of the
next millennium in the year 3000, the veils
between our realms will be gone and we will
all be able to transfer back and forth between
the earth and the afterlife just by thinking of
it and instantly adjusting our vibratory
frequency. You will no longer be imprisoned
in the physical density of your world. There
will no longer be any necessity to go through

the transition we call "death." You will no longer feel the loss of loved ones who decide to move into the afterlife, for you will know you can visit them any time you please, and they can come back to visit you.

Know I am with you in spirit when your thoughts come searching me out. Even if you didn't know me when I was living my lifetime as Susan Wells, we are still one in spirit, and I am pleased to assist you in any way I can.

Remember also, you are assisting me by your living. It is as though you are all great teachers who are demonstrating how to live a human life. As you meet and move through your challenges, we in the afterlife learn from them just as you do. I hope you can come to realize how far-reaching your influence is in this universe. I know it is difficult for you to see in your present state of consciousness, focused as it is on earthly events. But it is apparent to me, now that I have this new way of seeing things.

When I died, I was ushered into a world I had no idea could be this beautiful and this joyful. In the coming millennium, I want you to know, a good deal of this beauty and joy that I speak of will be coming into your world too. You will see your creations burst forth from your minds with the same instant gratification found in the nonphysical realms of the afterlife. You will come to realize that all beauty and joy—in fact, the entire universe—emanates from your own being. So all you have to do is look within yourself and find everything you could ever dream of or imagine.

What is it you will find within yourself? It is the light that I found when I left my deathbed for the last time and took my own crescendo into infinity. It is always there. It shines like a beautiful star in all its brilliance and glory. It is a beacon for all to see, guiding them to their own light within. We are all made of that same light. We each have a constant and everlasting supply of it. And that light keeps getting brighter and brighter, until we think we're going to burst with ecstasy and joy at its warmth and love.

And that is what God is. God is the glorious light, love, and joy that resides within each of us. As God bursts forth into new states of being, so do we.

Epilogue

Am I glad I "died"? You bet! I wouldn't have it any other way. It has been a wonderful journey for me and an exciting adventure all the way.

Appendix:

Questions and Answers

Q   *If life is that great in the afterlife, why would anyone want to come back to earth, where there is much pain and suffering?*

A   There are many who greatly enjoy the physical reality offered on earth, and they reincarnate time after time after time. Judgments about breaking the cycle of reincarnation and ideas about karma that amount to, "You'll have to keep going back until you finally get it right," are simply not true for those beings. Instead, they see human life on earth as a wonderful opportunity.

In the overall scheme, the earth is a very beautiful world, and the human body is a wonderful vehicle with its sensations of sight, sound, touch, taste, and smell. It gives its inhabitants a wonderful opportunity to hold their creations in their hands, to touch them, to look at them, to admire them long after they have been created.

Those beings love the earth because they can feel—truly feel—their emotions with their physical bodies. When they feel sorrow, their eyes shed tears. When they feel anger, their bodies pump with adrenaline. They get the urge to jump up and down, to clench their fists, and to growl in rage. When they feel shame, their faces turn red, and when they feel joy, their eyes light up and their facial muscles break out in a smile. In the afterlife none of these emotions can be felt to the extent they can be felt on earth

Let's face it: There are long waiting lines for beings to get into available bodies so that they can experience the drama of human life because such experiences are—well, more *dramatic,* to say the least.

Q   *Do you celebrate holidays or engage in other ritualistic practices in the afterlife?*

A   We do both, but not necessarily for the same reasons you do, nor with the same effect. The rituals here—and the holidays, too—are far more spontaneous and made up on the spur of the moment. A group of beings might be gathered together, and there arises this desire to celebrate, so we'll have a party. Or there might be some who want to explore aspects of their spirituality, and they will undertake that exploration in a ritualistic manner.

It is not that the same exploration cannot be undertaken without the ritual, but that the ritual adds something to the exploration. Perhaps it adds beauty, or structure, or some mutual vibratory frequency on which to focus our attention as a group.

If you think about it, that is exactly the same phenomenon occurring in your rituals. Churches have devised rituals in their services to draw everybody's attention to the same place at the same time. They also do it to add beauty and structure, both of which give the participants greater comfort.

We find rituals are performed more often among those who have recently left human lifetimes, for they are recreating situations to make themselves feel at home. Thus the whole concept of building a house, creating a garden, adorning their new bodies with "clothing," and gathering together in groups to take orientation classes—all of these are rituals carried here from the earth and used until they no longer serve a purpose.

As we move away from the earthly concepts and our consciousness becomes more free flowing, we leave rituals behind. The reason is that the structure that ritual provides doesn't serve well in this unstructured environment.

Now isn't that a paradox! We spend our whole lifetime as human beings learning rituals in order to deal with space and time, linear thinking, and logical progressions. We then come to the afterlife and spend our whole "lifetime" here learning just the opposite.

And, remember, many of the rituals you perform in your life create wonderful memories in later years. If you think about it, life on earth as a human being is nothing but a series of rituals, one to the next. And isn't that beautiful!

Q   *Do you ever need to take a rest or go to sleep?*

A   Sometimes. As in your world, there is a temptation here to become so excited with all the new adventures and experiences that we can quickly overindulge and then be intoxicated by it all. As with your intoxication, we then have to drop back from all the excitement to sober up, so to speak. Otherwise, the feeling can be similar to being drunk. We soon lose control over our functions and it becomes impossible to move around in our outer world. The next thing we know, we're falling flat on our face, as it were, or even passing out. We then implode to a cocoon of energy where we can "sleep" it off and rebalance our energy.

This is as close as we come to having a sleep state or rest period here. For the most part, if we pace ourselves, we can go on for long periods without the need to rest.

Instead we find ourselves changing pace from high level activity to low level activity. Other times we move from being within a group to being "alone" within our own consciousness. In other words, we too have a so-called outer world and inner world just as you do. There are times—most of the time, I suppose—we are focused in our outer world, playing or talking or working or traveling with our friends here. Other times we sink back within our own energy and focus on our inner spirituality. This inner "self" is where we connect with the higher essence of our being, or what you would call God.

Q   *It seems as if everyone on earth is addicted to something. Do people carry their addictions into the afterlife? In other words, do you have addictions there, too?*

A   Here in the nonphysical realms of the afterlife we are not as plagued by addictions as on earth. For one thing, many addictions arise because of the unique biological and chemical attributes of certain physical bodies. Thus alcoholics have certain chemical reactions in their brains that cause them to crave more alcohol if even a small amount is ingested. Compulsive overeaters are known to have a more sensitive sense of taste and irregularities in their metabolic functions, causing them to be unable to stop eating when their stomachs are full. Drug addicts have a biochemical function that raises their immunity level so that greater and greater dosages are required to achieve the same effect. All of these lead to addictive behaviors.

Even the most solid of bodies we create for ourselves here in the afterlife are not the same physically and biochemically as the bodies we left behind. Thus, even in the so-called lower levels where the beings sometimes run amok, they are not doing so because of addictive behaviors. Even those who may have lain drunk all their lives, or smoked cigarettes until their lungs were eaten away with cancer, or overdosed on drugs, will find they soon give up their "drugs of choice" after they have been here a short time. One important reason is that the substances which abused their physical bodies on earth do not pack the same wallop on a nonphysical body. Then again, there is not the pleasure—or, more accurately, the avoidance of pain from withdrawal symptoms. Hence it is much easier to withdraw from chemical substances here without the often overwhelming effects of detoxification you find on earth.

The so-called social addictions, such as overspending, compulsive gambling, and various other obsessive/compulsive behaviors, are not experienced here either. For one thing, there is no need to overspend because such addictions usually derive from a belief in poverty and limited resources. Victims of these addictions are usually operating from a belief that there is never enough to satisfy one's needs. Here they quickly find out there is always enough, more than enough, more than anyone could possibly ever want. Thus, not feeling deprived anymore, they may feed their coffers for a short time with their particular activity of choice, but they will soon be satiated.

Many of the addictive tendencies on earth are really a sickness of the soul, a feeling of being cut off from the source of all life and a feeling of abandonment by God. Some unfortunate human beings have been so damaged in their early lives that they may go all through their adult lives feeling lost and out of touch with their spiritual nature. Believe it or not, many have chosen to experience such isolation and separation from their spiritual source. Experiencing such loss makes the reunion that much more joyful. When they finally come back home to their spiritual source, they no longer need to engage in such destructive behaviors as they did while ensconced in a human body.

You will probably notice addictive behaviors are almost exclusively the province of the human race. You don't see animals and plants going around engaging in self-destructive behaviors, only human beings. The reason is that plants and animals are always connected to the source of their being and go out into their world with that knowledge and awareness.

As you know, addictive behaviors have always plagued the human population all the way back to the days when human beings lived in caves. There were gambling, compulsive overeating, drug addiction, alcoholism, addictive sexual behaviors, and codependent relationships back then too. You believe addiction is more rampant in modern times, but you simply have chosen to make yourselves more aware of it and have access to the technology which displays it to you on your TV every day.

Q   *What are angels, and how do they fit in?*

A   Many of you believe that angels are
      specific beings or personalities, rather
      like a particular species that has been
      given a job by God to watch over you.
      And if that is what you believe, that's a
      beautiful way to see it, for the angels do
      not mind how you happen to perceive
      them.

      In truth, the angels represent a
      particular vibratory frequency in the
      consciousness that we know as God-
      All-That-Is. We are all connected to the
      angelic realms because we are all
      connected to God. Therefore it is more
      accurate to say that each of you has a
      portion of your consciousness that
      reaches into and through the angelic
      realms, just as your consciousness
      reaches to God.

      Because you are playing with the idea
      of individuality in your excursion on
      the earth as human beings, you would
      naturally be more comfortable depicting
      the angels as separate beings you can
      identify and name. And it is perfectly
      fine if you choose to do that.

What is their role? Anything you want it to be. If you want someone to watch over you and to protect you from danger, they will do so. If you want guidance in your daily living, you will receive it. If you just want an invisible friend to talk to or to be your companion when you feel lonely, then all you have to do is to ask. If you don't choose any such assistance and prefer to manage your life by yourself, that is fine too. No one, angel or otherwise, is going to intrude or meddle in your life if you don't want.

But if you do want to add a little magic and joyful energy to your daily living, then the angels will be delighted to oblige. And if you choose to see your angelic friends as chubby little cherubs or as fairy-like winged creatures, then they will be whatever you want them to be. In the end it doesn't matter because the angelic consciousness is a part of your own consciousness anyway. You just don't see it that way because you are used to seeing your own consciousness as more closely aligned with your own physical body and mind. In truth, your consciousness stretches out to encompass the entire universe.

Q   *Do you still use names in the afterlife?*

A   When we first arrive here we still use
     names to identify ourselves, especially
     in the more solid levels where the
     lifestyles are reminiscent of the life-
     styles we just left behind on earth.
     Most, if not all, of us will use the name
     we had in our most recent earth life,
     but we could choose any name for
     ourselves if we wanted to.

     After we have become acclimated here,
     and especially after we have begun to
     evolve to the less solid forms in which
     we communicate by mental telepathy,
     names become redundant. Beings who
     come up to me don't have to ask me my
     name because they already know who I
     am. Otherwise they would not be in my
     presence. Similarly, I don't necessarily
     associate others I see with their names.
     I can merely blend with their energy
     and know everything there is to know
     about them, so why bother with a
     name?

     You see, names are a human invention
     because human beings love to go
     around labeling everything in their

outer world. You don't feel comfortable if you don't know the name of everything in your environment. You even give names to your pets, though they truly don't use names in their lifestyles either. Moreover, they certainly don't care if you have a name or not. You're just *you*. In other words, they know who they are and they know who you are, and that's all that is necessary.

But human beings love to play with intellectual concepts. You love to analyze everything, and you don't believe you can truly understand something if you cannot give it a name. It's almost as if it cannot exist unless it has a name.

All of this name giving is a function of your languages. Here in the afterlife we don't have languages either. We communicate by telepathy and we know all there is to know. So languages—and names, which arise out of the use of languages—are redundant. In short, no, we don't use names here after we've been here a while.

But then, when you think about it, you didn't use names when you first arrived on the earth as little babies either. After you were born you became acclimated to the lifestyle on earth, and the first thing you learned was your name, and then a few words for other familiar objects. Before you knew it, you had organized your consciousness within the structure of language. So now it is difficult for you to comprehend how anyone could get along without names and language. But they can. We do so all the time here in the afterlife.

Afterword

fter reading about the afterlife from Susan's point of view, you may be thinking to yourself, "Yes, that's all well and good for *her*. But how do I know if that's what happened to my brother, Charlie?"

Or if you know of someone who is facing their own death right now, how can you be sure Susan's experiences will apply to them? Or to *you* when your time comes? The only way you can know for sure is to ask. Ask your own loved ones who have passed on to tell you what happened to them. Ask your loved ones who are getting ready to cross over if they would be willing to stay in touch with you.

Does the idea of communicating with the dead seem outlandish to you? It shouldn't. Recent surveys have shown as much as 53% of those surveyed have acknowledged some form of contact with a deceased loved one. Others have done so, and so can you, if you will only give it a try. You have nothing to lose by trying and everything to gain if you succeed.

I have found it is easier to establish contact with a deceased loved one if we both have agreed to do so and have worked out the logistics before the loved one passes on. But I would caution you, in approaching anyone who you know or suspect is dying, don't be pushy. There is nothing more disconcerting to those who are battling a life-threatening illness than to have their loved ones talking about their demise and pushing it in their face before they are ready to deal with it and accept it themselves. If you approach them too aggressively or too soon, they may rebuff you and shut you out. Instead, simply be observant and let them lead the way.

In my experience, the best thing we can do for loved ones who are terminally ill is to develop and use our listening skills. I try to let them talk about what is on their mind, and I am willing to listen to anything they want to say. This means listening with an open mind and an open heart. Then I focus on what they are telling me and draw them out even more with encouraging words and gestures. I never disagree with anything they say, but instead seek to understand what they are telling me. Above all, I try not to judge what they say. Even if what they say does not ring true for me, I know it rings true for them.

On the other hand, I am never surprised if they change their minds and switch back and forth between different moods. I realize they are sorting out their own feelings and attempting to understand what is going on themselves. When faced with a serious illness, most people will flip back and forth between hope and despair, believing one moment they are conquering their ailment, and then giving up the battle in the next moment. They will skate back and forth between wanting to live and wanting to die. They may be terrified of dying but feel exhausted by the struggle to survive. They will deny the severity of their condition in one moment and beg to be released from their pain in the next. We may wonder if they are coming or going, and they may be wondering the same thing.

I never point out the inconsistencies in their words or feelings, but allow them to feel whatever they are feeling in the moment. Always, I try to be supportive, whether they are angry, sad, elated, desperate, or even oblivious.

When we listen without judging, we are establishing and building trust. We are allowing our loved ones to feel safe in opening up to share with us what is going on inside. If they come to trust us and know we won't contradict or ridicule or minimize or be frightened by what they have to say, they will open up even more to us. After I have created a bond, I find I can gradually move to a place where I may ask questions and even share my own feelings eventually. But, at first, I believe it is extremely important to allow this connection with the dying to be focused completely on them instead of on me.

When I first approached Susan Wells with the idea to remain in contact after her death, I had already known her for almost three years and had known for more than six months that she was dying. I had learned from listening to her on many occasions that she had come to an acceptance of her situation and was open to new ideas. Before I even asked her if she would be interested in contacting me from the other side, I knew already she would say yes.

It is important to spend as much time as possible with loved ones before their transition into the afterlife. This time spent together serves many purposes. First, the bond of love that develops between you before they leave enhances the connection and increases their ability to reconnect after they have gone. You will then be better able to sense their presence because you will have become familiar with the subtle nuances of their personality. After sitting with them week after week, feeling their energy in each encounter, you will have less doubt that their attempts to contact you afterwards are real. You will *know* it is them because you will feel their same familiar energy. I have found that the strongest and most long-lasting contacts from loved ones in the afterlife have been with people with whom I had formed the strongest bonds before they died.

If it is not possible to set the stage for contact before a loved one dies, all is not lost. There have been many instances of reported contacts with loved ones from beyond the grave without any preparation beforehand. After all, they may die suddenly in an accident, so their death may come as a complete surprise or shock. In other cases, you may have already lost a loved one in the past and the idea you could communicate with them did not seem possible to you until this moment while you're reading these words. In all cases, however, my experience has been, the greater the emotional bond, the more likely there will be contact.

There may be times, as Susan has mentioned, when contact with the deceased may not be possible. For example, when Susan was undergoing the "incubation" period she described in Chapter Four, I lost contact with her for eight days. I have known others who did not reappear for many months. There are some who may go into a state of suspension similar to a coma because they did not believe in any life after death. It could take months or years for them to wake up again. On the other hand, your loving thoughts projected to them may be the very thing that knocks on their consciousness and wakes them up to an awareness that they are still alive. So don't give up. As with many other situations in life, persistence often pays off.

There are many different ways to establish contact with loved ones in the afterlife. What will work for you may not work for another. It will be your job to discover what works best for you. Some people will actually see an apparition, especially when it is dark. Others will see flashing lights or dark spots flickering out of the corner of their eye. Sometimes you will be jolted awake by someone appearing in your bedroom. In fact, I have had so many contacts in my bedroom from loved ones and strangers alike that I am no longer startled when I find them marching into my bedroom, standing at the foot of my bed, or even sitting on my bed. I have also had apparitions of balloons dropped on me, flowers handed to me, phantom cats and dogs pouncing on the bed, and all sorts of other strange occurrences to attract my attention. If they can't attract my attention this way, they will often start showing up in my dreams.

I have found that loved ones who have been trying to reach me succeed most often at night when it is quiet and I am alone. This is a time when there is the least amount of distraction from my work life and my social life. I have read we are most receptive to paranormal phenomena just as we are falling asleep and waking up as our brain waves are moving through the alpha state. A quiet meditative state also seems to provide the greatest receptivity for the same reason.

I have noticed water enhances the opportunities for contact, such as when standing in a warm shower, swimming laps in a pool, washing dishes, or sitting on a lonely beach and watching the waves come in. Perhaps it's not the water itself. Perhaps any activities that quiet the mind and draw us away from our hectic daily lives will do.

Sometimes you may hear someone's voice, or you may hear strange sounds around your house. I once heard a loud creaking noise in the headboard of my bed about fifteen minutes after I turned off the light to go to sleep. Night after night, this loud creak would occur, and it went on for several weeks until I finally realized someone was trying to attract my attention. At last, when I acknowledged the signal they were giving, the creaking stopped and we went on to a more conventional (and less noisy) form of communication. I never did figure out how they were able to make that loud creaking sound night after night.

You may be tempted to discount anything that does happen as only your imagination. Often the encounter will occur so quickly that you may doubt it even happened at all. Other times, especially if you see or hear something strange, you will wonder if you are just making it all up in your own mind. You are in good company if you feel this way. I have felt this way many times. Even Susan Wells believed at first that her out-of-body experiences into the afterlife were just hallucinations. What finally convinced her, and will convince you too, was the repetition.

For this reason, it is a good idea to keep a tape recorder or a note pad next to your bed at night so that you can keep a record of any encounters, strange occurrences, or dreams. Otherwise you may forget all about it by morning. When I have gone back later to read my "Bumps in the Night Journal," I have been amazed at how frequently these events have occurred. Most of the time I would not have remembered these contacts the next morning had I not recorded the incidents as soon as they occurred.

When one of those strange incidents occurs, I have learned not to judge it. Instead I try to remain detached and just observe it until it disappears. Then I write it down as best I can remember it. After that I let it go. The next time something strange happens, I write that occurrence down. Soon I find a pattern in the events and I can then come to believe those events are not imaginary.

One of the reasons encounters with the deceased feel imaginary is that our loved ones must first attract our attention before they can begin to communicate with us. They often find it easiest to attract our attention by doing something strange. Otherwise we might not pay attention at all. As soon as they grab our attention, say, by flashing past the corner of our eye, our first response is often to go into our left brain and try to analyze what has just occurred. We will turn our head quickly to the place where we saw the flash and we will see nothing there. End of incident. Almost immediately our logical mind will take over and say, "There is nothing there. Ergo, I didn't truly see anything. It must have been just my imagination." We've just convinced ourselves it never happened. And then we quickly forget about it.

The only way to know for sure if these incidents are imaginary or real is to continue to observe them. If you write them down each time they happen, you may find the incidents occur with greater frequency over time. If you notice this greater frequency, and if the incidents become more and more obvious over time, then you may be sure someone is trying to attract your attention. The surest way to encourage them to keep trying to make contact is to openly acknowledge their efforts: "Was that you, Gertrude? If it was, I hope you'll try again to reach me."

If you have recently lost a loved one, keep in touch with others who were close to him. Share your experiences and ask others if they have encountered any strange incidents. More often than not, the recently deceased will be going around trying to make their presence known to everyone they were close to. If more than one of you notices these incidents, then they are more likely to be real than imaginary.

The resistance and doubt is mostly on our side of the veil. As Susan Wells has mentioned, the recently departed can still see us and can move around in our environment. If you ignore them or discount their attempts to attract your attention, then they will eventually give up and go away. But if you truly want to communicate with them, they will keep trying until you establish a communications link. If you are unsure that any particular incidents are your loved one's attempts to contact you, then all you have to do is to ask for assurance and proof. In most cases she will be able to give you information only you and they could have known so that you will know for sure the contact is real.

Once you have established contact with a deceased loved one, the fun begins. You will be able to satisfy your curiosity about their lifestyle and to obtain any other information you desire. You may simply engage in a conversation with them by mental telepathy. If you ask them a question, the answer will immediately come back to you in your mind.

A disadvantage to this method of communication, however, is that you may quickly forget the information they have conveyed to you. There were many times when I would be doing something mundane like taking a shower, and I would think about Susan; she would show up immediately, ready to start a conversation. I would be thinking about something she had said in one of our previous sessions, and she would then start in on a discourse on that topic. The words would come gushing through my head and go running right down the drain with the water, to be lost forever. Startled, I would yell out, "Wait a minute, Susan! Hold that thought until later when I can sit down at my computer." But when I finally had a chance to sit down at the computer for a session with Susan, I would never know if she had been able to recover all those profound thoughts I had let slip down the drain.

The best way to engage in communication with the deceased is by "automatic writing." Automatic writing takes no special skills. It is simply a process of recording what your loved one has just told you so that you may have something tangible to read later on. You may choose many different methods to record the words. Some people simply sit down at a table with a pencil and paper. Others use a computer. Still others dictate the words into a tape recorder, and they may then later transcribe the tape. Experiment with different methods to see which one works best for you.

I have tried all the above methods and have found advantages and disadvantages with each. Pen and paper are simple, but I find the information comes through more clearly if I close my eyes. In trying to write with my eyes closed, I sometimes cannot read my writing afterwards. With a tape recorder I become distracted by my own voice, or else I have trouble switching back and forth between receiving the words and then recording them. Moreover, I always feel as though I'm interrupting the transmission. But then I have never been any good at dictating correspondence into a recorder either.

For these reasons, I prefer a computer. I learned to touch type in high school, so I feel most comfortable sitting at my keyboard with my eyes closed. Most computer keyboards have a little bump on the "F" key and the "J" key, so that I can keep my fingers on the correct keys. As I'm typing away, the computer will automatically wrap to the next line and go to the next page when necessary.

I have even worked out little editorial conventions with my pen pals in the other realms. For instance, Susan Wells loves to emphasize words, so she instructs me to type "ital" after words she wants me to italicize. She also often starts on a train of thought and then changes her mind in mid-sentence. When she wants me to strike the existing partial sentence, she tells me to hit the "J" key three times. Then she goes on with her dictation. Later I search for "JJJ" in the text and delete the errant tangents.

By focusing only on the words as they flow into my brain, I can detach from what is being said and keep the mechanical and editorial portions of my mind out of the way. Later I can come back and fix any typographical errors before printing the document.

If you are not very good on the keyboard, you may accomplish the same result with voice recognition software. Instead of typing, you simply repeat what you hear as the words flow into your consciousness. With this method, however, it is important to keep your eyes closed so that you don't become distracted by the words appearing on the monitor as you speak them. Otherwise each time the voice recognition software gets the words wrong, you will lose the connection with your deceased loved one. After you have finished a session, you can always go back and fix the errors. You can also ask your deceased loved one to stick around and help you by repeating what he had said when you run across words that don't make sense.

If you want to gather information from a loved one in a systematic manner, then you will need to schedule time for your automatic writing sessions. Ruth Montgomery sat down at her desk each morning at 8:30 sharp. After ten to fifteen minutes of meditation to reach the alpha state, she would begin her writing session and then stop abruptly at 9:00, unless a ringing telephone or other household noise interrupted her sooner. She believed it was unsafe to channel the information from her spirit teachers for more than fifteen minutes.

Jane Roberts and Robert Butts tried to schedule Monday and Wednesday evenings after the dinner dishes had been washed, but they skipped sessions whenever more pressing matters occurred. Jane would sit down in her favorite rocking chair and patiently wait for Seth to come through while Robert settled down on the couch opposite Jane. Her sessions were nearly always interrupted for one or two short breaks in which she would grab a beer, smoke a cigarette, go to the bathroom, or deal with a pouncing cat. On the other hand, many of her sessions with Seth would often go on for two or three hours or more.

As a hopelessly incorrigible night person, I often wait until near the midnight hour, and I have never been successful adhering to a rigid schedule. Instead I prefer spontaneous sessions, often on the spur of the moment, sometimes after I have been prodded all evening by Susan. If I were to attempt an automatic writing session in the morning, I am sure I would fall asleep during the session. For me, my neighborhood is quiet late at night. Cars have stopped rushing up and down the street outside, birds have stopped chirping, neighborhood dogs have stopped barking, and we almost never have thunderstorms in San Diego to play havoc with our tranquility, not to mention the electrical service. Also, in this modern era, when telephone answering machines can be set to quietly catch incoming calls and VCR's can be programmed to tape favorite TV shows, it is easy to schedule automatic writing sessions without feeling we are missing out on life.

Careful consideration should also be given to the place for automatic writing sessions. A quiet place with no possibility of interruptions is best. Other household members and pets are definitely a hindrance, so a quiet spot away from the household hubbub must be found. Your spouse and children must be trained to give you the privacy and quiet that you need, or else you might have to wait until they all go to bed.

Household pets seem to be attracted to the energy of deceased loved ones and always know when they are hovering around your house. My cats, who graciously allow me to share their house with them, will not leave me alone when Susan is around. They become excited by Susan's energy and want to jump into my lap to get as close as possible to it. Therefore I have to feed them and put them to bed for the night before I can sit down for an automatic writing session.

There are times, however, when interruptions cannot be prevented. If I am interrupted, I sometimes end the session and reschedule for a quieter time. Other times I deal with the interruption and then finish the session. I don't know how she does it, but Susan seems to be able to reestablish the connection very quickly whenever we have been interrupted. There have even been times when one of the neighborhood dogs has started barking in the middle of a session, and I have asked Susan if she could do something about it. Suddenly the dog stops barking, as though Susan has gone out there, connected with the dog's consciousness, and calmed the dog down. The next thing I notice is that it is quiet once more and Susan is busy dictating away. Thus I have learned to ask Susan for assistance in order to minimize the interruptions. It's true, I swear. But please don't ask me how she does it. "It's just magic," she says with a smirk and refuses to elaborate more than that.

Many people adopt various rituals to prepare for an automatic writing session. Most rituals are designed to achieve relaxation and focus of attention on the task at hand. Because she did not have to personally deal with the transcription of Seth's words, Jane Roberts merely sat quietly in her rocking chair with her eyes closed and waited until Seth moved in and blended with her own energy. She often would mention she could feel him close by just before she suddenly fell into a deep trance. But she also practiced automatic writing and was able to achieve sufficient contact with the American psychologist/philosopher, William James, and the French artist, Paul Cezanne, to publish books transmitted to her by each of them from the afterlife.

Though the majority of both books was received while sitting at her typewriter, Jane Roberts wrote that portions of *The Afterdeath Journal of an American Philosopher* were also scribbled down while she was sketching pictures, washing dishes, watching television, and taking naps. Moreover, she managed to receive much of the James material while her house was being renovated, hammers were banging, and workmen were wandering in to ask for water.

On the other hand, Ruth Montgomery practiced a more formalized ritual. She started each session with a silent prayer for protection from evil forces. Then her teacher, Lily, drew a lily and signed his name to let her know of his presence before embarking on his writing for the day.

I personally have never believed in any evil forces in the universe, so I feel prayers for protection are unnecessary. If all is of God, then all is safe in God's universe, I believe. But if you believe otherwise, then you might feel more safe and comfortable asking for protection or asking for only the highest good of yourself and the being with whom you are connecting. There seems to be a universal law that no one may connect with your energy without your express permission, and I have always relied on this law to feel safe. In all my years of communicating with entities in the other realms, friends and strangers alike, I have never had a negative or frightening experience.

Before starting an automatic writing session, I first sit down at my computer and start my word processing program. Once the computer is set up, I generally rest my hands gently on the keyboard, lean back in my chair, close my eyes, and start with ten or fifteen deep breaths to relax and to calm down the rambling thoughts in my mind. Soon I notice myself moving into a dark tunnel that seems to spiral downward as I go into deeper states of relaxation. Sometimes I will have slow moving, relaxing new age music playing softly on the stereo. Other times I prefer total silence. Often, as Susan moves in to connect with me, I feel a buzzing energy inside my right ear, and then I feel a liquid-like energy oozing into my body. This energy slowly makes its way down my arms and out through my fingers just before words begin to flow into my brain.

As soon as the words start flowing through my brain and out through my fingers, I start to see pictures and scenery. Sometimes Susan will appear in those scenes, other times she is invisible or just a glowing light. Most of the time I will lose all sensation of my own body sitting in the chair; I will instead begin to feel as if I am floating and undulating in midair.

There have been times when I have been more tense from a stressful workday and then have had more difficulty connecting with Susan at the beginning of a session. At those times it seems as though Susan is very far away and I can't reach her. When that happens I call on my spirit teacher, Ardrith, to assist us. Then I feel Ardrith's energy step into the center and act as a transformer device that boosts Susan's energy level so that I can feel it more strongly. I usually receive a vision of Ardrith plugging two electrical cords together.

At times while he is connecting Susan and me together, Ardrith will move his own energy through me and say a few words. Once the writing has started, I can then relax and not worry as much about the connection. Then Ardrith will say, "Here is Susan now," and the writing goes on in Susan's words with no more feeling of interruption than the starting of a new paragraph. At other times Susan has started the session as she normally does, and then she has finished with, "And now Ardrith is here and he wants to tell you something." The next thing I know, Ardrith is dictating without skipping a beat.

My automatic writing sessions with Susan or Ardrith generally last between a half-hour and two hours. I lose all track of time and am always surprised to come back and discover how much time has elapsed. I rely on Susan or Ardrith to control the timing. It feels to me that they are monitoring my energy level and they conclude the session when my energy level winds down. This does not imply that automatic writing is tiring. In fact, I usually feel relaxed and regenerated after a session. But because I schedule these sessions late at night, I'm always concerned about going to bed at a decent hour so that I can get up the next morning.

As I mentioned in the Preface, there are times when the demands of my work prevent me from sitting down for an automatic writing session with Susan, sometimes for months at a time. During those times I stay in practice by setting aside some time each day to meditate. I also maintain contact with Susan by mental telepathy and carry on conversations with her as I'm going about my daily activities. I have also found that channeling and automatic writing are skills that are never forgotten once they have been learned. Even after long absences from my automatic writing sessions, I have found to my amazement that I pick it back up right where I left off.

To achieve the proper state of relaxation in order to communicate with loved ones in the afterlife, I also highly recommend the Hemi-Sync tapes and the training programs offered by The Monroe Institute in Faber, Virginia. Originally developed by Robert Monroe and described in his three books, *Journeys Out of the Body*, *Far Journeys*, and *Ultimate Journey*, Hemi-Sync is a patented process that uses sound technology to balance your right and left brain so that you can more easily reach the higher levels of consciousness where communication with the afterlife takes place. You can even use The Monroe Institute programs and tapes to explore the afterlife yourself. For further information, you may visit their web site at http:// www.monroeinstitute.org.

One of the greatest advantages deriving from these skills is that it maintains an ongoing relationship with our loved ones who have gone into the other realms beyond death. While others have mourned and grieved the loss of Susan Wells, I have felt no loss at all. Instead our friendship has grown deeper and more profound as the years have passed. She is a constant companion who blesses me with her love and caring. She has taught me that friendship does not require the physical presence of someone. This lesson has carried into my relationships with friends and loved ones in this life. Even when I can't spend time with them, I can send them loving thoughts and receive their love in kind. Even when I am alone, I never feel lonely, for I have learned I am never truly alone.

Susan also provides me with a great deal of help in my work. She seems to have access to all the great legal minds. If I tap into "The Dead Lawyers Society" whenever I encounter a problem or need advice, Susan and her colleagues enable me to write brilliant legal documents and to give eloquent oral arguments in the courtroom. Time after time I have seen stubborn and recalcitrant IRS agents cave in and give me and my clients everything we have asked for in tricky settlement negotiations. Call it magic. Call it miracles. Call it inspiration and intuition. Call it what you will. My life has been greatly enhanced by maintaining friendships with my "friends in high places."

And when she is not busy helping me create the adventures of my life, Susan still sits down with me regularly to tell me of her own adventures in the afterlife. She continues to explore the mysteries of the universe and to share with me what she has discovered. In due course we will publish a sequel to this book.

If you would like to participate in our next book, we invite you to write to us. Perhaps you have questions about something Susan has discussed in this book. Perhaps you have wondered about something Susan did not address here. Susan says she will be happy to entertain questions of general interest about the afterlife and about life in other realms of the universe.

On the other hand, Susan has asked me to tell you to please not ask certain kinds of questions. First, she would prefer not to give specific advice to solve your personal problems. We are all given our share of problems to solve in order to achieve spiritual growth and we need to seek our own inner guidance.

Similarly, she cannot heal our physical ailments. Instead, we all need to listen to our own bodies and seek the assistance of trained health care professionals that we are led to by our own inner guidance.

Susan also does not care to become a fortune teller or to forecast our individual futures. We are here to learn how to create our own reality, and subscribing blindly to psychic fortune telling simply gives away our power to do so.

For the same reason, Susan would prefer that you not ask, "Where is my Aunt Hazel, who died last year?" Instead, she would encourage you to contact Aunt Hazel yourself. Most likely, Aunt Hazel is hovering around you waiting for you to open up to her attempts to tell you where she is.

Finally, Susan does not wish to engage in any discussions or arguments about dogmatic or religious beliefs. She believes there is a kernel of truth in every doctrine or belief, and arguing about whether one faith is better than another completely misses the point. No matter what anyone else believes to be true, we are each a unique aspect of God and therefore have a unique perspective of the Truth. We are each discovering and rediscovering the truth as we go along.

Regrettably, it may not be possible for us to respond individually to every letter we receive.

But if we do publish your question in our next book, we will gratefully acknowledge your contribution, and we will send you an autographed copy of the book as an expression of our appreciation.

You may write to me at the following address:

Harriet H. Carter

c/o Hillbrook Publishing Company, Inc.

PO Box 3308

San Diego, CA 92150-3308

If you prefer, you may contact me through the Internet. My E-mail address is:

HCarter33@HillbrookPublishing.com

And Susan pops in at this point to say that you may, of course, contact her as well through any of the means we have just discussed.

Susan Wells and I both give you our best wishes and kindest regards.

Harriet H. Carter

San Diego, California

Index

Order Form

Postal orders: Hillbrook Publishing Co., Inc., PO Box 3308, San Diego, CA 92150-3308

Telephone orders: (858) 675-8111

Fax orders: (858) 675-8114

Email orders:

orders@HillbrookPublishing.com

Please send _____ copies of *"Guided Tour to the Afterlife," by Harriet H. Carter as told by Susan E. Wells*. I understand I may return it for a full refund for any reason, no questions asked.

Please send FREE information on:

❑ Other books ❑ Speaking/Seminars

Name:_____

Address:_____

City:_____State:_____Zip:_____

Country:_____

Telephone:_____

E-mail:_____

Cost: US $16.95 each

Sales tax: Please add 7.75% for books shipped to California addresses.

Shipping:

US: $4.00 for first book and $2.00 for each additional book

International: $9.00 for first book and $5.00 for each additional book.

Payment: ❏ Check   ❏ Money-Order

❏ Visa   ❏ MasterCard   ❏ Discover

Card
number:_____

Name on
card:_____

Exp. date:_____

Thank You!